an introduction to the

nineteenth edition of

the Dewey decimal

classification

an introduction to the nineteenth edition of the Dewey decimal classification

C D BATTY
BA FLA

CLIVE BINGLEY LONDON

14128

First published 1981 by Clive Bingley Ltd
16 Pembridge Road, London W11 3HL
Set in 10 on 12 point Press Roman by Allset
Printed and bound in Great Britain by
Redwood Burn Ltd., Trowbridge, Wiltshire.
Copyright © 1981 C D Batty
All rights reserved
ISBN: 0-85157-303-7

British Library Cataloguing in Publication Data

Batty, C. D.
 An introduction to the nineteenth edition of
 the Dewey Decimal Classification
 1. Classification, Dewey Decimal — Programmed
 instruction
 I. Title
 025.4'3   Z696.D8

 ISBN 0-85157-303-7

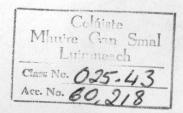

AUTHOR'S NOTE

This book began as the first of a number of texts used in the research
begun in the College of Librarianship Wales into the applicability of
programmed learning techniques to education for library and information science. The original purpose of these texts was to test the
suitability of the programmed textbook in various forms for certain
kinds of tuition. In formal programs, their purpose is to acquaint
students with the mechanics of classification and indexing systems outside the classroom, thus allowing class time to be used for discussion
and further investigation. Beyond this, the books may be used for in-
service training and continuing education beyond the scope of formal
programs.

Reviews of previous versions have called for a history and account
of the scheme. Although the original design of this textbook did not
include such a section, I have included a foreword in this version that
gives as succinct an account as I can quiet my conscience with. Otherwise it would have been another book.

Few can be more aware than the author of the book's imperfections.
In the 'author note' to the programmed text on the sixteenth edition
of the *Dewey decimal classification* a hope was expressed that
comment and criticism might improve future editions, and grateful
thanks are due to those readers whose interest, sympathy and under-
standing helped to improve the text in revision. Inevitably, however,
these revisions and the changes in recent editions and now in DC19 have
necessitated a completely rewritten text, and the ever generous help and
advice of colleagues and students alike is here gratefully acknowledged.

Particular thanks are due to Mr Benjamin A Custer, Editor of DC
for many years, a good friend and a fine editor, and to Mr John H
Humphry of Forest Press, for their constant help and advice. I should
also like to thank Dr John Comaromi, the new editor of DC, for his
most helpful comments on the present version.

David Batty
University of Maryland

5

FOREWORD

Previous editions of this programmed introduction to the Dewey
Decimal Classification have been concerned solely with the mechanics
of number building in the scheme. Published reviews and personal
communications have frequently recommended the inclusion of some
historical background and general description. The remarks that follow
are a personal and affectionate view of a scheme that the author has
worked with closely all his professional life.* He teethed (as it were)
on the 13th and 14th editions, grew up with the 16th, and has explored
the 17th, 18th, and 19th with several generations of students. He has
even enjoyed a detailed retrospective bout of practical application with
the 7th and 9th editions.

The Dewey Decimal Classification is one of the most interesting
phenomena in the history of librarianship. Its nineteen editions span
almost the whole of the organised development of the profession; it was
the first scheme that professed to be for all libraries; its outline has
barely changed from the beginning, and yet today it is used, and used
satisfactorily, by more libraries than any other scheme. (In all fairness,
we should admit the claims of the Universal Decimal Classification,
DC's nephew, but evidence is lacking for a final judgment.) It supports
one of the largest and best organised national bibliographies, the
British National Bibliography, and it has been used in a computerised
SDI experiment in public libraries in Lake County, Indiana. It has
undergone constant and sometimes radical revision from within, and it
has been translated, adapted, augmented, and supplemented by libraries
all over the world. Through all vicissitudes it has remained structurally

*The serious student can find the history of the scheme in John P Comaromi's
The Eighteen editions of the Dewey decimal classification, and detailed description and analyses may be found in the standard textbooks on classification and in
the *Encyclopedia of library and information science*. John Comaromi, now editor
of the Dewey Decimal Classification, is at work on an explanatory textbook.

7

recognisable and consistently useful. It has been criticised for being simple, for having sometimes lengthy notation, and for lack of detail. Yet these are faults that may be the source of its virtues. The lore of DC is that its initial strength and popularity were founded in its simple decimal notation, and in the Relativ Index that enabled classifiers at different times and in different places to classify in the same way. These may have been attractive features at the time (they are still), but I think that the abiding success of DC was due to two other features, implicit even in the first edition, that anticipated problems and theoretical solutions fifty years later. These features gave the scheme an unsuspected inner strength. Before we explore these features, let us look at the origin and development of the scheme.

Melvil Dewey was a strong-minded man of considerable intelligence who had devoted himself to education. He had been a young assistant teacher in upper New York State and went on to study at Amherst College in Massachusetts. There he worked as a library assistant and proposed a classification scheme for the library. At that time libraries customarily devised their own classification schemes, assuming that their unique collection, user community, and possibly even library architecture demanded it. It is difficult for us now to realise just how radical was Dewey's proposal for a scheme that would organise not only Amherst College's collection but also that of any other library and, moreover, organise it not by the conventional fixed location of general subject areas within which books had fixed addresses, but by relative location, in which the book would move as the collection grew, but would always remain in the same position relative to other books on the subject. Even the great Edward Edwards of the British Museum library had proposed, in his *Memoirs of libraries*, only a model scheme to be the basis of other libraries' schemes, that would expect to add their own fixed location within the subject organisation.

In his prefaces, Dewey claimed intellectual descent from the scheme of Battezatti in Italy, a scheme for booksellers derived from the justly famous scheme used and modified by the great Paris booksellers (which had also influenced Edward Edwards), and of W T Harris of the St Louis public schools, who claimed that his scheme was an inversion of the scheme of Francis Bacon. There is no real evidence that Dewey had access to Battezatti's scheme and the resemblance to Harris' scheme is clear only at the most general level. In recent years there has been a suggestion (dismissed fairly conclusively by Comaromi) that Dewey had access to a scheme prepared for the arrangement of the 1876 Centennial

8

Exhibition in Philadelphia. In fact the level of classification concerned is very general: a linear arrangement of a handful of more or less independent disciplines. Many schemes in Dewey's day recognised these disciplines and their arrangement was often a kind of intellectual exercise, pleasing to a classificationist like Henry Bliss, but whose internal structure would have far greater impact on the organisation of knowledge in libraries. Probably Dewey's claims of intellectual descent were more cosmetic than real.

On the other hand, Dewey claimed the decimal notation for his own, the product of contemplation on the scheme during a Dean's sermon in chapel. Yet decimal notation had already been used in at least the well-known scheme from Princeton, and the principle of fractional division within decimal notation was fairly well demonstrated, even when applied to fixed location schemes.

The first edition of DC in 1876 was a modest booklet of some forty pages, only ten of which were the scheme; the rest were divided evenly between Dewey's preface and the index. It arrived at an opportune time; public and small college libraries were growing, and their libraries seized on a ready-made and comprehensible scheme. Dewey's second edition in 1885 was ten times the size of the first edition, including instructions for augmenting topics in one class by adding detail from another class, and instructions and tables for general subdivision by place and form. The second edition also contained major structural changes, and the outcry from librarians who used the scheme was so great that Dewey promised an 'integrity of numbers' policy that would preserve the main structure, and allow changes and extensions only within established classes. That policy was maintained from 1885 to the 14th edition of 1942. The result was a fundamentally sound, but overgrown scheme: a spare nineteenth century New England frame, with layer upon layer of twentieth century indulgence of detail.

Some editions were classic, used even after later editions appeared; in between were some editions that included accretions of detail. One reason for this was the reluctance of Dewey's editors and advisors (Dewey had given up direct editorship after the third edition) to include any new topic hastily. About each such edition, Dewey himself often announced that there was little but minor updating, but that a new edition was needed because the previous edition had sold out. Dewey ordered modest printings; he seems always to have viewed the scheme as an anxious parent views a musically gifted child, not yet realising that the child has grown up and actually has played at

9

Carnegie Hall and the Royal Festival Hall.

By the 14th edition the scheme was decidedly ramshackle. It was big, in some areas lopsided, and it looked old-fashioned. Melvil Dewey had died, and the scheme was technically in the charge of the Library of Congress, Decimal Classification Office. A new editor was appointed to bring out the 15th edition. This was expected to be the Standard Edition (the name chosen for the 15th edition). The new and typographically attractive two-volume edition contained a castrated scheme. Only a quarter of the 14th edition detail remained; alphabetical listing predominated over systematic at the most detailed level; the Library of Congress philosophy of literary warrant prevailed, so that if the Library of Congress owned fewer than ten books on a topic it disappeared from the scheme; and major subject rearrangements violated Dewey's 2nd edition promise of an 'integrity of numbers'. The profession expressed an objection to the 15th ('Standard') edition even livlier than they had to the 2nd edition, and with commendable haste Forest Press and the Library of Congress found a new editor, Benjamin A Custer, to bring out a back-to-the-14th edition as soon as possible.

Custer has been possibly the finest and most sensitive editor of DC since Dewey himself. His work on the 16th through the 19th editions has met, accepted, absorbed, and made use of the most significant challenges and contributions of classification theory in the history of DC: the structure and methodology of faceted classification and the use of facet analysis. As a result, DC has made sense of and has expanded its earlier subsidiary tables and 'divide like' devices into a set of seven tables of auxiliary topics and a system of 'add' devices that reflect and can express many aspects of complex topics, even though DC is not a faceted scheme, and only partially now a synthetic scheme.

To understand the nature of synthetic and faceted classification schemes we must go back to the last years of the nineteenth century.

Classification in the general sense was, up to the mid-nineteenth century (and for many amateurs is still), an hierarchical arrangement of *things* in a family tree arrived at by division by successively appropriate characteristics. This philosophy of classification works for simple disciplines like botany or zoology or chemistry; it does not work in the world of books, where a single book may be described by a *thing*, a *process* happening to it, an *agent*, a *tool* of that process, and perhaps the combination of several of these.

In 1895 a conference at Brussels recognised the many aspects needed to describe non-book materials, and it agreed that a new and detailed classification was needed to organise a file of new, ephemeral materials and also to be the consistent basis for national bibliographies of conventional and unconventional materials of all countries. The conference established an International Institute for Bibliography and agreed that the DC should be the basis of the organisation of the file. DC was chosen because it was already document oriented, it could be expanded infinitely, and it had the widely understood decimal notation. The Institute tried for the next two decades to maintain a single decimal classification: Dewey's scheme for monographs and general libraries, and the 'Brussels scheme' for special materials. In the end, the intransigence of Dewey's staff, who saw any deviation from Dewey's own work as heresy, caused the Europeans to break off and develop the Universal Decimal Classification (UDC). It appeared first in French in 1928-33, and immediately began translation into English and German. Further discussion of the UDC can be found in standard textbooks and also in the *Encyclopedia of library and information science*. In later years DC has incorporated a few ideas from UDC, but the two schemes remain separate.

UDC's ideas of synthesis were expanded by S R Ranganathan in the second quarter of this century when he realised that existing classification schemes did not respond to logical desiderata or criteria. He developed his own scheme, the Colon Classification, initially using the punctuation mark, the colon, derived from UDC, to link details from different aspects of subjects. These different aspects (or *facets*) of subjects were mutually exclusive clusters of topics reflecting the same characteristics of division: the PERSONALITY or ENTITY ASPECT of a subject (*BUILDINGS* in BUILDING); MATTER (*BRICKS* in BUILD-ING); the ENERGY or PROCESS ASPECT (*CONSTRUCTION* or *FINISHING*); the AGENT ASPECT or the PLACE and TIME ASPECTS etc. Each of these are developed in a faceted classification as mini-hierarchies, and detail taken from any or all facets relevant to a subject may be assembled into a single class number not hitherto enumerative. Beginning with the 17th edition some principles of faceted classifica-tion have been acknowledged in the development of the DC.

DC now contains several components: the prefaces by Dewey and the current editor; the tables of subdivision; the current schedules; and the index. Since the 17th edition each new edition revises at least one but at most two complete schedules at the two-digit level, eg 510 MATHEMATICS (18th ed), 150 PSYCHOLOGY (19th ed). These are

11

called *phoenix schedules*. Further, since the 18th edition, the tables of subdivision are applied more generally, thus making the scheme more generally synthetic.

Such is the scheme today. Its structure and supporting syntax, and its auxiliary tables reflect the principles of modern classification theory. However, they are founded on those abiding features I mentioned in connection with the very first edition but did not elaborate on. To my mind Dewey's instinctive incorporation of these features provided much of the strength of the internal organisation of the scheme.

The first of these features concerns the recognition of multiple characteristics in a subject area. Whenever a subject may be divided by more that one characteristic, the array or arrays derived from the *most general* characteristic are listed first, and other arrays by characteristics in increasingly specific order. For example, in 630 AGRICULTURE, the first section contains farming in general, the second lists diseases etc, and the third lists specific crops. This arrangement is very natural, since instinctive shelf or systematic catalogue arrangement is from general to specific. However, a book that combines two of these ideas, eg DISEASES OF TOMATOES, should combine them in specific/general order (TOMATOES – DISEASE), to place the book at its specific topic. DC, like most classification schemes now, contains frequent instruction to divide specific topics by the detail of an earlier general array in the same subject; indeed 630 AGRICULTURE is a good example. This simple and obvious idea has been explicit and widely accepted in classification and indexing only since the early years of this century; there are hints in Cutter's 1876 *Rules for a dictionary catalog*, but they do not result in the clear and consistent construction of complex subject headings, as can be seen from the Library of Congress List of Subject Headings. Yet even in the first edition of DC we find the general to specific listing of arrays, in 400 LANGUAGE, 630 AGRICULTURE, 900 HISTORY etc. Further, in 400 LANGUAGE Dewey listed specific subdivisions within individual languages that made explicit combination in the *entity/process* order described above. 423 ENGLISH DICTIONARIES is formed from 420 ENGLISH LAN-GUAGE and 413 LEXICOGRAPHY. Simple and general though this is, it anticipated by a generation the explanations of classification theory, and provided a sound basis for growth.

The second strong internal feature is the 'divide like' device, now called 'add'. Obvious to us now, it was not so obvious as an innovation. Dewey only hinted at it in the first edition, but made it explicit in the

12

second. There are two ways of extending any topic: by the addition of detail from a separate table of subdivision, and by the addition of detail from another class ('divide like'). Even the tables of subdivision in DC, from the earliest to the present day, have their roots in the 'divide like' device. The Standard Subdivisions reflect the GENERALIA class; the Area Tables sprang from detail in HISTORY; the newer tables for the subdivision of LANGUAGE and LITERATURE were until recently the 'divide like' organisation within those classes. In the preface to the first edition of DC, Dewey remarked that although the printed schedules limited division to the 3-digit level, the application of the scheme at Amherst had already produced 4-digit and 5-digit notations. He pointed to 550 GEOLOGY in which 554/559 contained the geology of the several continents, eg 554 GEOLOGY OF EUROPE, and suggested that the detail given in 940 EUROPE in HISTORY could be used to extend 554. In a totally enumerative scheme, and a generation before the UDC, Dewey anticipated synthesis.

Despite its origin in a college library, DC has become known as a public library scheme. It was so known even at the turn of the century when the stacked deck of Charles Martel and J C M Hanson produced a hands down judgment in favour of an in-house scheme for the Library of Congress. Actually, many academic libraries in the US did use it until the largely irrational 'flight from Dewey' reclassified even the Melvil Dewey Memorial Library in New York State by the Library of Congress scheme. Outside Dewey's own country, acceptance was rapid and world-wide in English speaking cultures. Brown's 1906 *Subject classification* held a thin red line in some of England's public libraries until mid-century, but at last hearing only the reference library in Rotherham remained as the last bastion, and DC reigns all but supreme. Not a few academic libraries in England and in other English speaking countries use it, it is the organising scheme of the *British National Bibliography*, and it is included in machine-readable bibliographic services like OCLC and RLIN.

DC's future looked precarious at the time of the 15th edition; since then its development has been steady and probably the sounder from the incorporation of some facet analysis. It stands ideologically or theoretically between its two major counterparts: decidedly more flexible than the Library of Congress classification, and certainly simpler than UDC. The international exchange of machine-readable bibliographic information should provide a setting for DC to thrive, since it emphasises some fundamental characteristics which Dewey gave his creation: simplicity of use, the capacity for articulation, and the reflection of a conviction that not all the world is contained in one library.

INTRODUCTION

This book is intended to teach you the rudiments of practical classifi-cation with one classification scheme: Dewey's *Decimal classification*, nineteenth edition. It is not intended for use with any other classifi-cation scheme, even though the devices and methods discussed are of general validity.

The *Decimal classification* is a work in three volumes: the introduc-tion, followed by the supplementary tables for the scheme; the main schedules arranged in the order of the classes of the scheme, together with their numerical notation that gives the scheme its name; and the alphabetical subject index, called a 'relative index'.

You should have a copy of DC19 by you as you work through this book, and you should use it not only to solve the problems but also to check the examples and see how the scheme works.

This book is a 'scrambled textbook'; ie its pages are not read conse-cutively and indeed are not numbered as pages at all. Instead, the lessons and problems are divided into *frames* and these are numbered boldly for easy reference. On the first page (frame 1) you will be given the first step of the course and at the bottom of the page you will find a question on the information you have been given. You will be offered a number of solutions to the question, only one of which is correct. If you choose the correct answer you will be directed to the next step of the course; if you choose the wrong answer you will be directed to an intermediate step where you will be shown your mistake and given more instruction. A further question will offer you the opportunity of proceeding to the next main step of the course. If at any time you wish to look again at a particular part of the program you may do so by means of the *Concept index*. An alphabetical index to the examples to be classified appears at the back of the book.

Now turn to frame 1 and begin.

CONCEPT INDEX

16

1 The basic operations for finding a class number for any topic are always the same. First analyse the topic so that you know what the *specific* topic is, what discipline it belongs to, and what extra aspects may be involved. Then translate that analysis into the notation of the scheme, according to the structure of the classification.

For example A GEOLOGIST'S GUIDE TO THE CHEMISTRY OF SULPHUR should be analysed as SULPHUR; ITS CHEMISTRY; A GUIDE; FOR GEOLOGISTS.

So the translation of the analysis begins by looking for SULPHUR, in the discipline of CHEMISTRY, and it may be possible to add subdivisions for GUIDE and GEOLOGISTS.

If you already know the scheme very well, you may be able to go directly to the right places in the schedules and pick out the right notation, and if your topic is a complex one, you may also be able to assemble different pieces of notation in the correct way. But until you know the scheme as well as that, you should use the index to guide you to the right place in the schedules, in some cases choosing from a number of possible places laid out for you in the index. Melvil Dewey himself always recommended that even if you could go directly to the schedules you should always scan the index—just in case an aspect existed that you had not thought of.

Now analyse the following topic, choose the most specific term, and look in the index for it. Then turn to the frame shown by the answer. Do this even if you realise when you look at the index entry that you should have chosen something else. You will get a second chance in the frame you turn to.
REINFORCED CONCRETE
REINFORCED turn to frame 6
CONCRETE turn to frame 3

2 Careful!

This is a programmed or scrambled textbook—you have just turned to the *next* page. You should turn to the *frame* indicated by the answer in the problem you have just looked at.

Now go back to frame 1 and look at the problem and its answers again.

---

3 No

You chose too general a term; this is not about *all* CONCRETE, but specifically about REINFORCED CONCRETE. Notice in the index that CONCRETE is nearly always the specifying word in a phrase, whose other term alone would also have been general, eg CONCRETE BLOCKS, CONCRETE MUSIC etc.

 If you had looked under REINFORCED, you would have found
    REINFORCED
      CONCRETE
        ARCH CONSTRUCTION 721.04454
(though, of course, we are not concerned with the class numbers themselves yet).

Now try another
DIGITAL COMPUTERS
DIGITAL turn to frame 6
COMPUTERS turn to frame 9

4 Good

SABER is the correct term to look for, just as TOMATOES would have been in the previous example.

Now go to frame 16

---

5 Not much help at first sight

HEPATITIS has no mention of VITAMIN THERAPY and until you know the scheme well you might be doubtful that this was the right way to proceed.

Now look up VITAMIN THERAPY and then turn to frame 10

6 Good

Sometimes, of course, the specific term you have in mind will not be listed in the index. Then you must think of a synonym or of a more general term. In either case, when you do find a term in the index, you must check it in the schedules to see if it is as *precise* a term as you can find. Frequently, DC does include terms in the index that have no place in the schedules, either because they are synonyms, or because they are too specific to merit a place of their own in the scheme. For example VASSAL STATES has no place of its own, and the index refers you to DEPENDENT STATES, which actually has several places in the schedules.

Try looking for one yourself.

Remember, look for the entry in the index and turn to the appropriate frame in this book. Do not yet check anything in the schedules.
THE EMOTION OF JOY
EMOTION turn to frame 11
JOY turn to frame 15

---

7 Not really

You should know by now not to look under a general term. You should have looked under TOMATOES and found a chain of references that we will explain in detail in a moment.

Now try another example
THE SABER AS A WEAPON
SABER turn to frame 4
WEAPON turn to frame 14

8 Good

You realised that TECHNIQUES, or THEORY, are only ways of looking at the subject (forms of presentation) and that you should look first for the specific term—WELDING or DIGITAL COMPUTERS.

Now turn to frame 24

---

9 No

You are still choosing far too general a heading.

Go back to frame 1 and read the notes carefully—then work out the example again and see if you can understand why and how you should choose the *most precise term*. Then continue with the programme.

The index entry for HEPATITIS does not explicitly confirm that
VITAMIN THERAPY FOR HEPATITIS should be placed somewhere
there, but the index entry for VITAMIN THERAPY not only gives
its own general number but also says
   s.a. spec diseases
Later we shall see how number building under the instructions at
DISEASES in the schedules would give a number for VITAMIN
THERAPY FOR HEPATITIS.

   Sometimes a topic will have a specific place in the schedules for
one aspect in one class, but will be included in another class for
another aspect, only at a more general level. Further the topic may
have even more applications and occurrences in less closely related
classes.

   For example if we were looking for CATS AS AGRICULTURAL
PESTS IN FORESTRY PLANTATIONS we would find no mention of
it under CATS, though there is an entry. But CATS includes
   s.a. Felidae
and the entry FELIDAE includes
   AGRIC PESTS
   s.a. spec types of culture

Try this one
PRESERVING TOMATOES
PRESERVING turn to frame 7
TOMATOES turn to frame 16

11 Not much help was it?

You looked for EMOTION, and found EMOTIONS in ED PSYCH, PSYCHOLOGY and RELIGION, with a few other details and references—but no reference to JOY. That was because you looked at far too general a term.

Look up JOY, and you will find that indeed it is too specific a term to merit a place in the schedules, but it is listed in the index in order to guide you to SECONDARY EMOTIONS (a topic more specific than just EMOTIONS). At SECONDARY EMOTIONS you are guided to a number in PSYCHOLOGY that would include JOY—though it does not specifically mention it. As it happens, if you had stayed with EMOTIONS, and scanned the schedules at the number given there for PSYCHOLOGY, you would ultimately have been led down to the place we have found through the index entry SECONDARY EMOTIONS. But it is usually *quicker* to look for the precise term.

Try another one
HOW TO WEAR YOUR DIADEM (ie, DRESS CUSTOMS CONCERNING DIADEMS)
DRESS CUSTOMS turn to frame 13
DIADEMS turn to frame 15

---

12 Really!

You should not be looking at this page. You should know by now to look at the specific topic TOMATOES and not the general discipline PALEOBOTANY.

Look up TOMATOES in the index and turn to frame 20

13 No

You are still choosing the general term instead of the specific one.

DRESS CUSTOMS does not help you at all—though it would help you in the end if you traced the correct hierarchy down to the most specific point (which is not DIADEMS).

If you looked under DIADEMS the index would have guided you to JEWELRY, which lists DRESS CUSTOMS as one of its places.

Remember, look first for the specific term, to allow the index to lead you easily to the appropriate level.

Now turn to frame 15

---

14 Come now. You are *still* looking under the general term. Look up SABERS in the index. It has only one place: ART METALWORK, but it also says

 other aspects see Edged weapons

EDGED WEAPONS includes MIL ENG which would be the correct entry.

Remember: always begin by looking for the specific term, and use the references to guide you on from there.

Now turn to frame 16

Now we have seen how DC does actually include terms in its index that may be too specific to merit a place in the scheme, so that you may be guided to the correct place that you might not be able to find if you approached it from a very general level. JOY can be assigned a place in the scheme, in SECONDARY EMOTIONS in PSYCHOLOGY, even though the scheme does not give it a mention in a scope note at the class number.

Another kind of reference from a specific term that does not represent a specific topic is made from terms that may have many applications, or many occurrences. Very often this happens when the topic is really a combination of two simple topics. For example ELEMENTARY SCHOOL COUNSELLING is really a combination of COUNSELLING and ELEMENTARY SCHOOLS. If you look up ELEMENTARY SCHOOLS you will find only

> ELEMENTARY SCHOOLS
>> FINANCE
>> LAW
>>> etc

and if you look up COUNSELLING you will find only

> COUNSELLING
>> EDUCATION
>> LAW
>>> etc

but you will find

> *s.a. spec levels of ed*

In other words through ELEMENTARY SCHOOLS or ELEMENTARY EDUCATION you will be guided to a place in the schedules where you may find

> ELEMENTARY SCHOOL COUNSELLING   372.1 6

Have a look at one for yourself
VITAMIN THERAPY FOR HEPATITIS
VITAMIN THERAPY turn to frame 10
HEPATITIS turn to frame 5

16 Good

The entry at TOMATOES does not include PRESERVING, but it *does* include
    s.a. Vegetables
and VEGETABLES includes
    DOMESTIC PRESERVATION
which would be the correct starting point for finding and checking a class number for PRESERVING TOMATOES.

Sometimes the references can take you into further and different directions. Let us take TOMATOES a little further and look for
PALEOBOTANY OF TOMATOES

PALEOBOTANY turn to frame 12
TOMATOES turn to frame 20

---

17 Not really

You are still looking first for the word that represents the *form* of the document and as the index has told you, this is a *standard subdivision*.
    Distinguish between the subjects themselves and the form in which they are presented.

Now turn to frame 24

18 Well now . . .

The index entry ARRANGEMENTS includes FLOWERS, but at this point you would not know if FLOWERS could include TOMATOES. Of course the schedules themselves might help you, but we are still exploring how the index works.

If you want to check DECORATIVE, look it up in the index and turn to frame 25. Otherwise turn to frame 19.

---

19 And there we are

A final check at the index entry TOMATOES reveals the general reference
   other aspects see Plants
and at PLANTS we find the entry
      PLANTS
         ARRANGEMENTS
            DEC ARTS
   We have seen already what happens when two different components combine in what appears to be a single topic, like ELEMENTARY SCHOOL COUNSELLING.

How about
TECHNIQUES OF WELDING
TECHNIQUES turn to frame 21
WELDING turn to frame 24

As before, the entry TOMATOES does not have anything about
PALEOBOTANY, and we know from the last exercise that VEGE-
TABLES does not either. But we had not explored the other
reference
> *s.a. Solinales*

At SOLINALES, of course, we see immediately the entry for
PALEOBOTANY, and we could take off into the schedules from that
point.

But we still have not finished with TOMATOES.

Try exploring this one
TOMATOES IN DECORATIVE ARRANGEMENTS
TOMATOES turn to frame 19
ARRANGEMENTS turn to frame 18
DECORATIVE turn to frame 25

TECHNIQUES may have seemed to you to be a specific application or
problem within WELDING, but actually it is a very general term that
may be applied to any specific topic. It appears in the index simply as
> *s.s.*−028

that is, *standard subdivision* 028.

Terms like HANDBOOK, TECHNIQUE etc, usually represent a *form
of presentation*, and in DC notation may be added to the end of the
notation for a specific term. We shall see how this is done later.

Now try another example
THEORY OF DIGITAL COMPUTERS
THEORY turn to frame 17
DIGITAL turn to frame 8
COMPUTERS turn to frame 27

22 We have just completed a section in which you learned something about the structure and use of the index to DC19. This is important to save you time in using DC in the future, but you must remember that the index alone cannot provide you with class numbers for topics; you must always check with the schedules. Indeed, the index is constructed in such a way that many times you *must* look in the schedules, because the index provides you with only a general indication of a topic, whose applications and subdivisions are laid out in the schedules.

Now we can begin to explore the schedules themselves and begin to find and build class numbers. Use what you have learned so far about consulting the index. To begin with we shall look for simple topics, and use only those aspects of the use of the index that you learned first. The more complex features of the index structure will be useful later.

Now turn to frame 26

---

23 No

You have made the same mistake twice on this point.

Go back to frame 26 and read the lesson carefully. Then try the question again.

You realised that we should look first for the subject of the document rather than its form of presentation or the approach to the subject.
In the example, WELDING is the subject of the document, and TECHNIQUES is only the approach to the subject.

What we have done so far has concerned only the index. The rest of this book is about the main schedules of DC19, and particularly about the ways in which the auxiliary schedules and the number-building devices help you form complex notation to represent complex subjects. This part was intended to acquaint you with the structure and appearance of the index so that you can use it to help you to find notation in the schedules in the future.

Now turn to frame 22

---

25 That was no help, was it?

DECORATIVE includes very general terms like ARTS and SCULPTURE, but has no clue about what to do with TOMATOES.

If you wish to check ARRANGEMENTS, look it up in the index and go to frame 18. Otherwise turn directly to frame 19.

26 Now we can begin to classify

Many subjects are easy; they occur only once in the whole scheme
and they have an unmistakable class number. But whether or not you
approach them through the index you must *always* check the number
in the schedules. You should be able to tell if you have the right
number by looking at any notes there may be at that heading and by
looking at the numbers and the headings round about.

What is the correct number for
THE MINERALOGY OF JAMESONITE
549   turn to frame 40
549.3   turn to frame 33
549.35   turn to frame 38

---

27 What is this?

We used the example of DIGITAL COMPUTERS a few frames ago, and
realised that COMPUTERS is too general a term, and we should look
first under DIGITAL COMPUTERS as the specific term. If you can't
remember or understand this part perhaps you should go back to
frame 1.

If you feel you really understand why and how you should look for a
specific term, then go to frame 24.

28 No

You have chosen a place in the wrong subject field. When you looked up TASTE, you saw TASTE (SENSATION) and were led to QUALITY CONTROLS, FOODS, and then to 664.07. But that is not the SENSATION OF TASTE; there is an entry at TASTE that does lead to SENSATIONS–it is AESTHETICS.

Study the examples again to see why your choice of terms was wrong– and then turn to frame 30.

---

29 No

You have chosen much too general a place. Probably you looked up the general term GAS LIGHTING in the index and used the number given there.

   You might have read through the schedules for 628 (though they are much too long to make this a practicable way), and you might have found the right place: 628.95. It would have been better to have looked for SODIUM VAPOR LIGHTING, which has a number 621.3276 in ENGINEERING, but also a reference to PUBLIC LIGHTING. That would have led you to the right place.

Now try again
CLOSE-UP PHOTOGRAPHY
778   turn to frame 40
778.324 turn to frame 31

Quite often a phrase that is not in the index will, by the structure of language itself, produce a term that does appear in the index, simply by reversing the order of words.

In spite of the warnings of the last lesson there are many subjects that cannot be named specifically in an index, or be given specific places in the schedules, but for which the scheme can provide exact class numbers. These are often complex subjects, where a simple subject is given a particular aspect, or is presented in a special way, or is even subdivided into classes belonging originally to another subject. These aspects, forms of presentation or subject subdivisions are often found to apply not to one subject only but to several or even all subjects.

Here are some examples: a HISTORY of SCIENCE; the ECONOMICS of FARMING; an ENCYCLOPEDIA of MUSIC; the WILDLIFE of SCOTLAND; the influence of TELEVISION on the CINEMA.

What many schemes do in such cases, DC among them, is to economise on the size of the printed scheme, and help the user, by printing commonly recurring aspects and subdivisions once only, with instructions on how to use them again when necessary. Combining elements of the scheme (and their class numbers) in this way to represent complex ideas is called *synthesis* and any list or arrangement that allows it is called a *synthetic device*.

Which of the following phrases best describes *synthesis*?
The presence of two or more ideas to make a complex subject. Turn to frame 44
A list of aspects or subdivisions to be added to a simple subject to make a complex one. Turn to frame 35
The combination of parts of a classification scheme to represent complex subjects. Turn to frame 42

The added term in the *index* entry can always be used in this way to help decide which place to choose.

Of course, it is rare to find a title or subject phrase that corresponds exactly with the entry term in the *index*; you must formulate your own before you begin to search. This is not difficult; the *index* usually lists synonyms, and even if at the first attempt you cannot find anything near your specific term, a little rephrasing will often produce a reasonable approximation. In any case, remember that you can always look up a number you recognise as representing a broader, more general topic and search in the *schedules* at that number for the specific place you require. *Index* entries printed in bold type are headings subdivided in the *schedules*.

Class headings and names in the *schedules* often have synonyms or explanations in brackets or in small type; these can be of great assistance in interpreting your subject. Notice also the presence of explanatory notes—often called 'scope notes'—which are intended primarily to define the range and limits of the subject, but often include terms and names, and may mention the one you have in mind. Always read these notes very carefully.

For example ANIMALS WITHOUT BACKBONES could give you trouble if you look up either ANIMALS or BACKBONES in the index, where DC lists class numbers for the relevant individual fields but without showing us anything directly helpful. What you must do is translate the phrase ANIMALS WITHOUT BACKBONES into the more scientific INVERTEBRATES, which can be found without trouble.

Which of the following numbers is correct for
DECORATIVE HORN CARVING

788.41   turn to frame 37
681.8184   turn to frame 52
789.913684   turn to frame 43
736.6   turn to frame 39

32 No

You looked up GOLD and found a number in the general field of
ECONOMIC GEOLOGY, which is quite wrong here. Just because
GOLD is mentioned specifically in that class is no reason to use it.
The general field here is FOLKLORE, and although in 398.3 there
is no specific mention of GOLD there is a class for MINERALS IN
FOLKLORE that would include GOLD.

Now try
THE SENSATION OF TASTE
664.07   turn to frame 41
152.167 turn to frame 30
701.17   turn to frame 28

---

33 Nearly

You have found the right general field and you have moved down the
schedules to a much more specific heading, but it is one that could be
divided still further to give the exact number for this precise topic
that you will find listed there.

Now try another example
THE PHILOSOPHY OF INSTRUMENTALISM
144   turn to frame 23
144.5 turn to frame 38
140   turn to frame 40

34 No

You looked up SODIUM VAPOR LIGHTING and assumed that
621.3276 was as close a place as you were likely to find. You should
have looked further to see the reference to PUBLIC LIGHTING.

Now try this
CLOSE-UP PHOTOGRAPHY
778   turn to frame 40
778.324 turn to frame 31

---

35 No

A list of common aspects or subdivisions for addition to an appropriate
simple subject to make it complex is *not synthesis*, but the synthetic
device that makes it possible.. *Synthesis* is the process of joining the
parts of the scheme together, of adding the terms from that list, and
should be distinguished clearly from the list itself. *Synthesis* is the
operation; the *synthetic device* is the apparatus with which the operation
takes effect.

Which of these statements is correct?
Synthesis is the listing in a classification scheme of complex subjects
with common aspects or forms of presentation. Turn to frame 54
Synthesis is the combination of parts of a classification scheme to
represent complex subjects. Turn to frame 42

36 No

You looked up GOLD and accepted a number in the field of GOLD-SMITHING, which is entirely wrong here. Just because GOLD is mentioned specifically in that class is no reason to use it. The general field here is FOLKLORE, and although in 398.3 there is no specific mention of GOLD there is a class for MINERALS IN FOLKLORE that would include GOLD.

Now try
THE SENSATION OF TASTE
664.07   turn to frame 41
152.167 turn to frame 30
701.17   turn to frame 28

---

37 No

You have confused the meaning of the word HORN and the number you have found is the number for MUSIC FOR HORN. You should always check the schedules carefully to see that you have the right meaning and context of the index term you are dealing with.

Now try this
INCORRIGIBILITY IN CHILD CRIME
364.36   turn to frame 39
155.453 turn to frame 48

You will have noticed already that very often the index gives a second word or phrase after the entry term.   In many cases this merely defines the general field to which the entry term belongs and confirms you in your choice.   Frequently, however, a topic occurs in many different fields, as we suggested a few moments ago—for example LIGHTING occurs in BUILDING, ELECTRICAL ENGINEERING, ILLUMINA- TION ENGINEERING, PHOTOGRAPHY and several others.   These scattered but related topics are called *distributed relatives* and it is the job of DC's Relative Index to show this relation and help us to dis- tinguish the correct subject field to which our version of the entry term belongs by adding descriptive terms.

It is vital to use a class number in the correct main class; if, for instance, we had found a number for THE MINERALOGY OF JAMESONITE in LEAD GEOLOGY (where JAMESONITE belongs in its geological aspects) it would have been quite wrong.   You must *always* check not only that your class number is accurate but also that it is appropriate and in the right general field of knowledge.

What is the correct number for
SODIUM VAPOR LIGHTING IN PUBLIC AREAS

621.3276   turn to frame 34
621.324   turn to frame 29
628.95   turn to frame 31

Sometimes, in spite of all your efforts, you will fail to find either a
relevant entry in the index, or a specific place in the correct main
class in the scheme. This is because the subject you are concerned
with lies beyond the development of the scheme—it is too specific. In
this case you must find the closest general heading or class which
would, if developed, include your subject. As we have already noticed,
scope notes and explanations can be of great assistance in these cases.

For example 736.25 is the number for SAPPHIRES in the general
field of PRECIOUS STONES. The MINERALOGY OF SAPPHIRES,
however, belongs to the field of MINERALOGY; sapphires are only
one of a group of minerals of the HEMATITE GROUP, not all precious
stones, and they must share a number with rubies, corundum and
hematite. Indeed sapphires are not mentioned by that name in the
schedules, but in spite of this we must place them in the correct main
class. So for THE MINERALOGY OF SAPPHIRES, in spite of their
specific listing in 736.25, the more general heading of 549.523
MINERALOGY OF THE HEMATIC GROUP OF OXIDES is the best.

Beware! Do not be led astray by the presence of the specific term
you seek *in the wrong subject field*. As we have seen, it is most important to find a place in the correct main class, and it is no fault of yours
(or the scheme for that matter) if one class has been developed to
include one manifestation of a topic, when the class you are concerned
with has not been developed sufficiently to name the topic you are
trying to place.

Now choose a number for
GOLD IN FOLKLORE
398.3   turn to frame 47
398.365 turn to frame 30
549.23   turn to frame 45
739.22   turn to frame 36
553.41   turn to frame 32

40 Not quite

You have found the number for the general field, but you have not persevered either in the index or in the schedules to find the exact number for the specific topic.

Try again
INSTALLING DISHWASHERS
696.12   turn to frame 33
696.184 turn to frame 38
696   turn to frame 23

---

41 No

You have chosen a place in the wrong subject field. When you looked up TASTE, you saw TASTE (SENSATION) and were directed to QUALITY CONTROLS, FOODS, and then to 664.07. But that is not THE SENSATION OF TASTE; there is an entry at TASTE that does lead to SENSATIONS—it is AESTHETICS.

Study the examples again to see why your choice of terms was wrong— and then turn to frame 30.

One of the most frequent examples of recurrent aspects is the *form of presentation*. This can be both *physical*, as in the form of arrangement, like a dictionary, or concerned with the *approach to the subject*, as in its history. Form of presentation applies almost equally to all subjects, and a list of what DC calls *standard subdivisions* (our first *synthetic device*) is given at the beginning of volume 1; Table 1, on pages 1-13. These divisions can be added to any number in the scheme with a very few, clearly indicated exceptions. The dash is not included in the final class number; it shows merely that *standard subdivisions* must be used with a class number from the schedules. Otherwise they are added as they stand, so that the symbol 0, never used to represent a subject subdivision, indicates that the following digit shows the form of the work.

One of the standard subdivisions, —09 HISTORICAL AND GEO-GRAPHICAL TREATMENT, can also be extended to give geographical subdivision and we shall see how to use this later. For the time being we shall concentrate on the standard subdivisions that show the form of presentation.

To give an example of their use: the standard subdivision which indicates the DICTIONARY FORM is —03 and the number for ELEC-TRICAL ENGINEERING is 621.3; A DICTIONARY OF ELECTRICAL ENGINEERING TERMS is therefore 621.303. Again, the standard subdivision —09 represents HISTORY AND LOCAL TREATMENT and PIRACY is 364.135. A HISTORY OF PIRACY is therefore 364.13509.

Now find the number for
THE THEORY AND PHILOSOPHY OF THE MANAGEMENT OF MATERIALS

658.7—01   turn to frame 49
658.71   turn to frame 51
658.701   turn to frame 58
100.6587   turn to frame 46

43 No

You have mistaken the meaning of the word HORN, and you cannot have checked the number you selected in the schedules. The meaning of the number you have chosen is APPRAISALS OF RECORDINGS OF MUSIC FOR HORN!

Always check the class number in the schedules.

Now go back to frame 31 and try the question again.

---

44 No

The presence of two or more ideas in a subject makes that subject a complex one and more difficult to classify. It would be a very large and complicated scheme that listed in order as many complex ideas as the scheme's originator could think of (though there are some that try!). Most schemes content themselves with listing fairly simple ideas (and there are quite enough of them) and arranging them in their groups or classes. But most schemes also recognise that complex subjects exist, and where possible they allow numbers for different simple subjects or ideas to be joined to make complex ones. It is this kind of joining that is called synthesis. The commonest kind of synthesis occurs when a group of ideas is found to be common to a large number of subjects. This group can be written down once and given special notation to allow it to be added to any of the appropriate subjects. An arrangement of this sort is called a *synthetic device.*

Which of these sentences is correct?
Synthesis is the listing in a classification scheme of complex subjects with common aspects or forms of presentation. Turn to frame 54
Synthesis is the combination of parts of a classification scheme to represent complex subjects. Turn to frame 42

45 No

You looked up GOLD and accepted the number in the field of MINER-
ALOGY which is entirely wrong here. Just because GOLD is mentioned
specifically in that class is no reason to use it. The general field here is
FOLKLORE, and although in 398.3 there is no specific mention of
GOLD, there is a class for MINERALS IN FOLKLORE that would
include GOLD.

Now try
THE SENSATION OF TASTE
664.07   turn to frame 41
152.167 turn to frame 30
701.17   turn to frame 28

---

46 You are wrong

You have found the right number for both the class and the *standard
subdivision*, but you have not put them together in the right order. The
standard subdivision, as its name implies, is always a subdivision of
something else; this is not surprising since it usually represents an aspect
of the subject or the form in which it is presented. It can never stand
first, or, of course, by itself; it must always come after a class number.

Now try this one
THE THEATRE MONTHLY
050.792 turn to frame 63
792.5   turn to frame 51
792.05   turn to frame 58
792–05   turn to frame 49

47 No

You are nearly right, but 398.3 is for *all* real subjects of FOLKLORE
and is not specific enough. Certainly GOLD is not used in the index
to guide you here (though MINERALS is) and in any case you should
always read the whole of the class to make sure that you have the
right place. MINERALS is the best heading that will also include
GOLD.

Now try
THE SENSATION OF TASTE
664.07   turn to frame 41
152.167 turn to frame 30
701.17   turn to frame 28

---

48 No

You have chosen the wrong number, either by not checking it in the
schedules, or by not rephrasing the subject to the more useful JUVEN-
ILE DELINQUENTS.

Now go back to frame 31 and read the notes carefully. Then work the
problem again.

49 No

You should not use the whole of the *standard subdivision* including the dash. That is to show you only that the standard subdivision should be added to a class number from the schedules. Always leave out the dash and add the rest of the standard subdivision as shown in the list.

Now try again
CASE STUDIES IN LIBRARY REFERENCE SERVICES

722.02552	turn to frame 46
025.52–0722	turn to frame 63
025.52722	turn to frame 51
025.520722	turn to frame 58

---

50 No

You have ignored the instruction that tells you:
     636.8003-636.8009 standard subdivisions
DC includes this instruction because places in 636.801-.808 are used for special subdivisions for the aspects of cats and their care. The answer should have been 636.8003.

Now remember in future to read and follow DC's instructions and notes.

Now go on to frame 53

51 No

You have found the right numbers for both the class and the *standard subdivision*, but you have not put them together correctly. The 0 of the standard subdivision is an *indicator* to show what sort of subdivision is being used (ie not an ordinary subject subdivision) and it must therefore be retained.

PROGRAMMED INSTRUCTION (−077) IN STATISTICAL MATHEMATICS (519.5) is simply 519.5077.

Now try again
A HISTORY OF LITERARY FORGERIES

098.309   turn to frame 58
090.983   turn to frame 46
098.39   turn to frame 63
098.3−09 turn to frame 49

---

52 Wrong

You have confused the meaning of the word HORN, and the number you have found is the number for HORNS in the MANUFACTURE OF MUSICAL INSTRUMENTS. Though it is true that horns often have decorative work on them, the example here is intended to mean HORN as a material.

Now try this
INCORRIGIBILITY IN CHILD CRIME

364.36 turn to frame 39
155.453 turn to frame 48

53 You are right

One exception to the simple addition of *standard subdivisions* to a class
number in the way that we have seen already arises when that number
already ends in 0. In many cases of this kind you will find that DC
gives careful instructions and examples on the use of *standard subdivisions*. Always look for notes at any class number you choose and
read them carefully. But sometimes there is no instruction and then
you must work out the compound number for yourself. Unless there
is a contrary instruction there is never any need to use more than a
single zero to indicate a *standard subdivision,* so that already existing
zeroes may be deleted until only a single zero remains.

   For example, THE PHILOSOPHY OF EDUCATION entails the
addition of −01, the standard subdivision for PHILOSOPHY AND
THEORY, to 370 EDUCATION, but the answer is 370.1−not 370.01.
Only the single zero is needed to indicate the standard subdivision.
Similarly, A HISTORY OF TECHNOLOGY, using 600 and −09, is not
600.09 but 609. You can check both these numbers in the schedules
since DC prefabricates them to help the user.

Which of the following numbers is correct for
A HISTORY OF THE ZOOLOGICAL SCIENCES
599   turn to frame 55
590.9   turn to frame 62
590.09   turn to frame 59

54 No

You are still mistaken about the nature of *synthesis*. It is not the list of terms or aspects to be used, and it is not the prefabricated complex subject that sometimes finds its way into a classification scheme. It is simply the *combination of parts* of a classification scheme (in themselves probably simple ideas) to represent complex ideas.

Now turn back to frame 30 and read the lesson carefully before trying the question again.

---

55 Wrong

You remember quite correctly that when we add a *standard subdivision* to a class number that already ends in 0 we must take away the surplus zeroes, but you did not remember that one zero must be left to indicate that a common subdivision is being used. Otherwise the resulting number may be confused with a *subject subdivision* in the same class.

For example, to add –05 PERIODICALS to 610 MEDICINE deleting all zeroes is to get 615, which is not the number for MEDICAL JOURNALS, but PHARMACOLOGY AND THERAPEUTICS—one of the subclasses of MEDICINE. The correct answer is 610.5.

Now try again. What is the number for
A HISTORY OF METAPHYSICS
119   turn to frame 66
110.09   turn to frame 59
110.9   turn to frame 62

56 No

Like the standard subdivisions the 'Areas' notation must be added to
an existing class number and this is shown by the dash, which disappears when the area notation is used. WAGES IN FRANCE, for
example, is made up of 331.29 HISTORICAL AND GEOGRAPHICAL
TREATMENT OF WAGES and the area notation −44 FRANCE.
Since the instruction at 331.29 says 'add "Areas" notation . . .' it is a
simple matter to construct the number 331.2944−without the dash.

Now try again
SOIL AND SOIL CONSERVATION IN NORTH EASTERN INDIA
631.49541   turn to frame 65
631.49−541   turn to frame 64
631.499541   turn to frame 61

---

57 No

You have used the right area notation but you have chosen to keep the
dash shown in the area notation. This is only to show that area notation
cannot stand alone but must be added to an existing class number. In
use it disappears.

Now try again
URBAN FOLKSONG
784.41732   turn to frame 60
784.491732   turn to frame 72
784.49−1732   turn to frame 69

58 Good

Sometimes, for one reason or another, DC will include a special instruction in a class to use more than one zero for *standard subdivisions.*
There can be several reasons for this and we will come to them later.
For now, you should remember that you can use standard subdivisions anywhere if DC has no special instruction, and that then you should use the single zero shown in the table of standard subdivisions, but that if DC has a special instruction to use more, then you must follow it.

What is the number for
A DICTIONARY OF CATS
636.803   turn to frame 50
636.8003   turn to frame 53

---

59 No

You added −09 to the class number without any alteration, which gives you a number with two zeroes. But we said that except in very special circumstances *one* zero would be sufficient to indicate a *standard subdivision*, and if the original class number had a zero already (or even two) then we could take away the surplus zeroes until there remains only the one that we need.

Now try again. Select a number for
A DICTIONARY OF ARCHITECTURE
720.03   turn to frame 66
723   turn to frame 55
720.3   turn to frame 62

60 No

You have read the instruction wrongly. The area notation is to be
added directly to the base number for GEOGRAPHICAL TREATMENT.
The example of SCHOOL ENROLMENT IN RURAL AREAS should
not have the answer 371.211734, but 371.2191734.

Now try another
INDUSTRIAL RELATIONS IN THE AFRO-ASIAN BLOC OF
UNALIGNED COUNTRIES

331.09–17165   turn to frame 57
331.0917165   turn to frame 72
331.017165   turn to frame 69

---

61 You are wrong

You have added the correct area notation, but for some reason you
have chosen to add an extra 9. It is true that in DC the digit 9 is tradi-
tionally associated with historical, and consequently also geographical
treatment, but there is no need to do anything more than DC tells you.
At 331.291-.299 GEOGRAPHICAL TREATMENT OF WAGES, for
example, you are told simply to add the area notation to the base
number 331.29. There is no necessity to do any more than this, so
that the correct answer is 331.2944.

Now try this one
DESIGN IN SCANDINAVIA

745.449948   turn to frame 64
745.449–48   turn to frame 56
745.44948   turn to frame 65

Now you have learned how to use standard subdivisions let us look at another table of common subdivisions also in volume 1 of DC—
Table 2: AREAS. These are used to show division or limitation by place, ie geographical subdivision: general kinds of geographical subdivision like land forms, oceans, etc, followed by specific continents and countries.

Almost any class may need geographical subdivision at some time, but in many classes place is one of the important kinds of subdivision and DC gives specific instructions on what to do.

In 367 GENERAL CLUBS, for instance, we find 367.91-.99 allocated to GEOGRAPHICAL TREATMENT with the instruction
     Add 'Areas' notation 1-9 from Table 2 to base number 367.9

All we have to do to find a number for CLUBS IN SWEDEN is to add the area notation for SWEDEN −485 to 367.9 to get 367.9485 CLUBS IN SWEDEN. Again, 526.32 SURVEY BENCH MARKS may be extended by an area table number like −415 IRELAND to give 526.32415 SURVEY BENCH MARKS IN IRELAND.

Now find one for yourself
WAGES IN FRANCE

331.2944   turn to frame 65
331.29—44   turn to frame 56
331.29944   turn to frame 61

63 No. You have made the same mistake twice

You may have to use *standard subdivisions* many times in classifying
books and it is worth taking care now to get them right. All you have
to do is to select a class number for the subject of the book and add
to it the standard subdivision which represents its form. To do this
you leave out the dash and add the standard subdivision as it stands
including the 0 that shows that it is a standard subdivision and not
one of the subject's own subdivisions.

Now go back to frame 42 and read the explanation again carefully.
Then work the problem, keeping the examples and the explanation in
mind.

---

64 No

You have just made the same mistake twice and it is unlikely that you
really understand the nature and use of area notation.
   Table 2 gives a list of countries and places and some geographical
features, so that the notation can be added on instruction wherever it
is needed. At the moment we are thinking only of the cases where DC
gives a specific instruction to use *any* area notation, and in these cases
all you have to do is write the digits of the area notation after the
class number concerned.

Now turn to frame 62 again, read the explanation carefully and try the
question again.

65 Good

You have found the correct class number in the schedules and you added the correct area table number according to the instructions (without the dash, of course) to get the right answer. Now try another one, this time using one of the early, more general geographical divisions.

SCHOOL ENROLMENT IN RURAL AREAS
371.2191734   turn to frame 72
371.211734   turn to frame 60
371.219–1734   turn to frame 57

---

66 No. You have made the same mistake twice

Remember that unless the scheme gives you a specific instruction (as it often does—you should always read the notes under the headings very carefully) then you need only *one* zero to show that you are using a standard subdivision.

Now go back to frame 53 and read the lesson carefully. Then try the question again.

69   No. You have made the same mistake twice

Although you have answered one question on geographical subdivision correctly you probably do not understand the idea of it as clearly as you should. Table 2: AREAS includes both a list of countries (−3 to −9) and a list of physiographic features and regions (−1). All these subdivisions behave in just the same way, and are added under instruction to relevant class numbers.

Now turn back to frame 62 and read it again. Then answer the question, thinking about why you choose the answer you do, and continue the programme.

---

70   No

You have added the area notation directly to the class number although there is no instruction allowing you to do so. Where there is no instruction we have to use a standard subdivision to help us.

   Now, although we are actually using two kinds of subdivision at once, the −09 of the standard subdivision HISTORICAL AND GEO-GRAPHICAL TREATMENT has no real meaning here beyond showing that the next group of digits comes from the area notation to indicate geographical subdivision. This means that in effect we add −09 to any class number that does not already have an instruction to add area notation, and add the area notation after the −09.

HOTELS AND MOTELS IN NEW YORK STATE
728.509747   turn to frame 73
728.5099747   turn to frame 68
728.5747   turn to frame 79

67 No, you are wrong

In this class geographical subdivision is important enough to have
several places allotted to it and these places end in the digits used
already at the beginning of the area notation. Obviously then there is
no need to use the same digits twice, or to continue to use the 9 that
is often characteristic of geographical subdivision in DC. THE
MORMON CHURCH uses 289.34-.39 for geographical subdivision and
the 4-9 are the 4-9 of the area notation for various countries. When we
add 42 for ENGLAND AND WALES there is no need to repeat the 4
already in the class number and so the correct answer is 289.342. In
any case DC always gives the base number to which you may add the
subdivision notation.

Now try another example
NORWEGIAN PRINTS
769.94481 turn to frame 74
769.9481   turn to frame 75
769.981   turn to frame 71

---

68 No

Class numbers that have no instruction to add area notation directly
can still be given geographical subdivision by using the *standard subdivision* —09 HISTORICAL AND GEOGRAPHICAL TREATMENT
to introduce area notation. When you do this you have only to add
—09 to the class number and then the correct area notation, but you
do not need another 9.
    The number for SILVICULTURE, for instance, is 634.95 which has
no specific instruction to add the area notation, but if we add —09,
then we can use the area notation —495 GREECE to make the class
number 634.9509495.

Now try another
GOLD, SILVER AND PLATINUM MINING IN SOUTH AMERICA
622.3420998 turn to frame 79
622.342098   turn to frame 73
622.3428   turn to frame 70

You have realised quite rightly that in a class like this geographical
subdivision matters more than in many others and that DC therefore
gives over a number of the subdivisions of the class for this purpose.
This results in the omission of digits characteristic of this kind of
division, like 9, and it usually means a shorter class number. But you
have gone too far and left out too many digits. The intention of DC
in assigning for example, 289.34-.39 for MORMON CHURCH,
TREATMENT BY CONTINENT, COUNTRY, LOCALITY is
to use the 4-9 of that class number as the 4-9 of the area notation.
The 4 of 42- ENGLAND AND WALES must be present in some form,
whether we think of it as the 4 of 289.34 with the remaining 2 added,
or 289.3 with 42 added. In any case DC always gives the base number
to which you may add the subdivision notation.

Now try again
THE MUSIC OF FRANCE
781.744   turn to frame 75
781.7444   turn to frame 67
781.74   turn to frame 74

Sometimes not all the area tables are relevant for dividing a given class number and the instruction in DC may limit the area notation to be used. This sometimes looks a little confusing but it is just the same as the method we have seen already.

For example in 379 EDUCATION AND THE STATE geographical subdivision is put at the end as 379.4-.9 PUBLIC EDUCATION BY CONTINENT, COUNTRY (etc) with the instruction

Add 'Areas' notation 4-9 from Table 2 to base number 379

in other words the 4-9 of 379.4-.9 *are already* the 4-9 of the area notation so that PUBLIC EDUCATION IN INDIA is 379.54.

In all cases of this kind with any table of subdivisions (and we shall meet this again later) DC always gives the *base number* to which the notation from the table of subdivisions should be added. Sometimes it is the class number you are concerned with. But sometimes it is a part of it, and if this is the case DC will always make it clear just what you are to do.

What is the number for
THE MORMON CHURCH IN ENGLAND AND WALES
289.342   turn to frame 75
289.3942   turn to frame 67
289.32   turn to frame 71

73 Correct

Remember when you use this general kind of geographical subdivision
that DC may have made arrangements for geographical subdivision in
the class you have chosen, and you should read all instructions and
notes very carefully. If there is a subdivision already allocated for
historical and geographical treatment *you must use it* rather than use
the —09 standard subdivision extended by area notation.

What is the number for
BIRDS OF ANTARCTICA
598.209989   turn to frame 82
598.29989   turn to frame 78

---

74 No. You have now made the same mistake twice

There is no need to be confused by this use of area notation. It occurs
when geographical subdivision is important in a class and when several
subdivisions of the class can be given over to it, instead of confining it
to only one. When this happens we usually find that the subdivision
digits are the same as the digits beginning the area notation, so they
can be omitted, and in such cases DC will give you the base number to
which you may add the subdivision notation.

Now go back to frame 72 and read the explanation again carefully.
Study the examples and try the question again.

So far we have used area notation only on finding specific instructions in the schedules, but there are many numbers that may need geographical subdivision where no instruction is given at all. In cases like this we must return for a moment to the *standard subdivisions* and look at −09 HISTORICAL AND GEOGRAPHICAL TREATMENT. Although this is primarily a subdivision representing the historical approach to the treatment of a subject it can also introduce area notation to give geographical subdivision.

For instance 622 MINING ENGINEERING AND RELATED OPERATIONS has no special subdivision for historical or geographical treatment. A GENERAL HISTORY OF MINING would thus naturally be 622.09 and since the standard subdivision −09 contains −093−099 with the instruction

Add 'Areas' notation 3-9 from Table 2 to base number −09

we can specify MINING IN SOUTH AFRICA as 622.0968.

This use of −09 to introduce an area table number will work for any class number in DC that does not already have a specific instruction about geographical subdivision.

Now try this one
SILVICULTURE IN GREECE

634.9509495   turn to frame 73
634.95099495 turn to frame 68
634.95495   turn to frame 70

You have used too many digits to introduce the historical period. The
list in the tables in volume 1 of DC is intended to be used in straight-
forward cases just like any other notation from the standard subdivisions. This means that the −09 that begins the period number is
the 09 meaning HISTORICAL TREATMENT so that all you have to
do is to add the period number to the class number in place of the −09
HISTORICAL AND GEOGRAPHICAL TREATMENT.

Now try again
PUBLIC EDUCATION IN THE SEVENTEENTH CENTURY
379.20909032 turn to frame 81
379.209032   turn to frame 86

You are still trying to use the *standard subdivision* −09 and area
notation when there is no need to do so. DC gives specific instruction
and makes special arrangements in many classes for you to use area
notation directly and you must always read all notes and instructions
very carefully before you decide on your class number.

Now turn to frame 78 and continue with the programme.

You will have noticed by now that the *standard subdivisions* also include 0901-0905 HISTORICAL PERIODS. Note that these are *general* historical periods only, for use when no country or locality is specified. You will learn later how to add period subdivisions to countries. For the time being remember that this list of period divisions is for use without specification of country.

These historical subdivisions must always be used as given; they cannot be abbreviated as area notation sometimes can. For example, THE WINDS OF THE WORLD IN THE NINETEENTH CENTURY uses 551.518 and the standard subdivision 09034 NINETEENTH CENTURY to give the class number 551.51809034.

Which of these numbers is correct for
WORLD COMMERCE 1950-1960
380.1090945   turn to frame 76
380.109045   turn to frame 86

---

79 No. You have just made the same mistake again

The use of area notation with any class number that does not have specific instruction for its use is really very simple. Add the standard subdivision −09 to the class number and add the area notation directly to that.

Now go back to frame 75 and read the explanation of the reasons for this again. Then study the examples and try the question again with these in mind.

Note that as always DC gives the base number to which you should add the notation from the Languages Table. Occasionally (as we saw with 'Areas' notation) that base number is not quite the same as the class number you are concerned with. For example, in the same class as 039 ENCYCLOPEDIAS IN OTHER LANGUAGES you will see 034 ENCYCLOPEDIAS IN FRENCH, PROVENCAL, CATALAN, in which the instruction reads

Add 'Languages' notation 41-49 from Table 6 to base number 03

Note that the base number is 03 and not 034. This is because the 4 already exists as part of the Languages notation. So a FRENCH LANGUAGE ENCYCLOPEDIA is a synthesis of 03 and -41: 034.1.

What is the correct number for
THE BIBLE IN DUTCH

220.53931 turn to frame 89
220.533931 turn to frame 88

You are still using the whole of the standard subdivision as well as the —09 for HISTORICAL AND GEOGRAPHICAL TREATMENT. You must remember that the period divisions are themselves extensions of HISTORICAL TREATMENT and consequently already include 09 as part of the number.

Now go back to frame 78 and read the explanation again carefully and study the examples. Then try the question again, and read all the notes in DC as you work it.

82 No

You are using the 09 standard subdivision extended by area notation theoretically quite correctly, but in this class there is no need for it since DC has already provided places for regional treatment. In cases like this you must follow the instructions.

Now try again. What is the correct number for
PUBLIC EDUCATION IN WALES

379.09429   turn to frame 77
379.429   turn to frame 78

---

83 No

You are still making the same mistake.

The number to which you should add the language notation is the *base* number, not the whole notation of the class you are concerned with (which already includes the first digit of the language notation).

Now go back to frame 80, and read the instruction and try the problem again.

You are committing the basic mistake of *including* the dash which
is only DC's way of showing that this notation may not be used by
itself. Always omit the dash when adding the subdivision notation.

Try another one
THE SEMITIC RACES
572.892   turn to frame 94
572.8–92   turn to frame 96

You are trying to include the dash from the language notation which
is simply DC's way of showing that another number must be used as
a base to which the language notation is added. Just join the two pieces
of notation together, but leave out the dash.

Now try this one
ROMANIAN INSTRUCTION IN ELEMENTARY SCHOOLS
372.65591   turn to frame 80
372.6591   turn to frame 92
372.65-591 turn to frame 90

Standard and geographical subdivision are not the only kinds of sub-division to have their own general tables in DC. DC18 introduced three others of a general kind: of *persons*, of *language*, and of *racial, ethnic, national groups*. Like the standard and geographical sub-divisions of Tables 1 and 2, they can never be used alone, but must always be used with a number from the general or auxiliary schedules. When they were introduced, they could be used only on explicit instruction in the schedules. Now, however, Table 5: RACIAL, ETHNIC, NATIONAL GROUPS and Table 7: PERSONS may be used anywhere in the scheme provided there is no specific instruction to include their notation directly, using 088 and 089, respectively, as their introductory indicators—as 09 is used for Table 2. We will see more of their specific use later. Now we shall turn our attention to the tables that have special application.

First look at Table 6: LANGUAGES in volume 1 of DC. This gives a complete list of languages, and subdivisions from it may be used whenever you see an instruction to add LANGUAGES notation.

For example 372.3-372.8 SPECIFIC ELEMENTARY SCHOOL SUBJECTS includes 372.65 FOREIGN LANGUAGES with the instruction

Add 'Languages' notation 1-9 from Table 6 to base number 372.65

so that FRENCH AS AN ELEMENTARY SCHOOL SUBJECT is the synthesis of 372.65 and —41 and produces 372.6541.

Now try one for yourself
AN ENCYCLOPEDIA IN LATVIAN

039-9193   turn to frame 85
039.9193   turn to frame 80
039.193   turn to frame 92

87 No, you are wrong

The 'Persons' notation should be added *as it stands* to the base number shown in DC's schedules. To insert 0 simply to mark off the subdivision notation is unnecessary and wrong.

Try another one
BIBLIOGRAPHY OF WORKS BY BLIND AUTHORS
013.08161   turn to frame 93
013.8161   turn to frame 99

---

88 No

Because the range of notation offered for extension by a language subdivision begins at 220.53 you have added the language number −3931 DUTCH directly to it. But DC gives you the base number 220.5 for the addition of language notation, because the 3 is already included in the subdivision number, and the answer is therefore
    220.53931

Now try
SPANISH LANGUAGE SERIAL PUBLICATIONS
056.61   turn to frame 83
056.1   turn to frame 89

89 You are quite right

A similar variation in applying subdivision notation occurs when the
instruction tells you to use some but not all of the language notation.
This is for the same reason as using a different base number: because
only a limited range of language is involved, and quite possibly some
of the notation already exists.

For example, 038 [ENCYCLOPEDIAS] IN SCANDINAVIAN
LANGUAGES says

> Add to base number 038 the numbers following 39 in
> 'Languages' notation 396-398 from Table 6, eg SWEDISH
> LANGUAGE ENCYCLOPEDIAS 038.7

in which 038.7 is formed from the synthesis of 038 and 7 (from 397).

Remember that DC will always tell you the base number if it is
different from the class you are concerned with, and will also tell
you explicitly which pieces of notation to ignore and which to use.

Now go on to frame 95

---

90 No, you are wrong again

You are still making what is really an elementary mistake. DC tells you
exactly what to do; follow the instructions.

Now read frame 86 again and see if you can do better.

91 So far we have learned how to add form, geographical, or other subdivisions to an already satisfactory class number, but it is often possible to add on subdivisions of the subject itself that are not actually listed in that class. Bear in mind, however, that this can be done *only* according to an *add* instruction. This *add* device is used in several ways, but its purpose is really always the same: to economise on the size of the printed schedules and thus save the time and patience of the user in using them.

It is the same kind of thing in use as adding an area notation to a number under instruction, but instead of taking a number from a special table, you take it from a class where enough detail has already been worked out for your purpose.

Generally speaking there are three types of *add* device. A class can be extended by numbers taken from (a) the whole classification (b) another class within the same subject field (c) a similar class in another subject field.

Take (a) first. This is the easiest form of the device and it occurs usually when a class can be divided by any object or idea that exists. For example, in 704.94 SPECIFIC SUBJECTS IN ART, after a list of subjects frequently chosen by artists, DC includes a class for everything else, at 704.949, and says:

Add 001-999 to base number 704.949 [etc]

Thus the REPRESENTATION OF AIRCRAFT TYPES (which is 629.133 in ENGINEERING) is 704.949629133.

Now try this
A SPECIAL LIBRARY ON NUMISMATICS
737.026 turn to frame 105
020.737 turn to frame 109
026.737 turn to frame 102

92 No

You have quite properly tried to add the language notation to the base number but because the last digit of the base number is the same as the first of the language notation you tried to suppress one of the repeated digits. This is quite wrong. DC tells you to add the language number as it stands.

Now try again
ALBANIAN PROVERBS
398.991991   turn to frame 80
398.91991   turn to frame 90

---

93 Good

You will have noticed that on the first page of Table 7: PERSONS you are instructed at the centred heading
▶ 03-08 PERSONS BY VARIOUS NON-OCCUPATIONAL
CHARACTERISTICS
that unless other instructions are given, you should class complex subjects with aspects in two or more subdivisions of this table in the number coming last in the table, eg
GIFTED UPPER MIDDLE-CLASS JEWISH MALE ADOLES-
CENTS -0829 (*not* -0622, -055, -041, or -03924)
Such an instruction reflects the acknowledgement by DC19 of the existence of the aspects or facets of a subject represented explicitly in a faceted classification scheme. The enumerative nature of DC tends towards the selection of the most significant aspect to provide a class number. Here the schedule has listed the aspects in increasingly significant order, so that the latest number must represent the most significant aspects. In other classes DC19 may display a *table of precedence* to indicate which aspects should be selected as being most significant.

Now go to frame 91

The last of the tables of general subdivision is Table 7: PERSONS,
described by physical and mental characteristics, by social, sex or
ethnic characteristics, or by their interests or occupations. Like the
tables we have just seen, this table may be used only on explicit
instruction by DC, or through the interposition of -088 from Table 1,
with any appropriate number from Table 7.

For example, 940.31503-.31587 RELATION OF VARIOUS . . .
PERSONS TO [WORLD WAR I] — CLASSES BY VARIOUS NON-
OCCUPATIONAL AND OCCUPATIONAL CHARACTERISTICS
includes the instruction

Add 'Persons' notation 03-87 from Table 7 to base number
940.315

so that MUSICIANS IN THE WAR would be formed from 940.315
and -78 to form 940.31578.

Now try one of these for yourself.
What is
CUSTOMS OF BLACKSMITHS

682.3904   turn to frame 98
390.4682   turn to frame 93
390.40682   turn to frame 87

Now let us look at another table of subdivisions—Table 5: RACIAL, ETHNIC, NATIONAL GROUPS, on pp 408-417 in volume 1 of DC.

This notation is used in the same way as the language notation, but this time to indicate peoples. If you have been used to using earlier editions of DC and you are now finding out about DC19 you will notice that RACIAL, ETHNIC, NATIONAL GROUPS are used to specify people where editions of DC before DC18 had to use a kind of language subdivision. Do not confuse Table 5: RACIAL, ETHNIC, NATIONAL GROUPS in DC19 with Table 6: LANGUAGES.

For example, in the main class LIFE SCIENCES, 572 HUMAN RACES has a subclass 572.8 SPECIFIC RACES with the instruction

Add 'Racial, Ethnic, National Groups' notation 01-99 from Table 5 to base number 572.8

so that a number for THE RACES OF EAST AND SOUTHEAST ASIA is formed from 572.8 and —95 to make 572.895.

What is the correct number for
SLAV RACIAL PSYCHOLOGY

155.84—918   turn to frame 84
155.84918   turn to frame 94
155.8418   turn to frame 100

---

96 No

You are still making the same mistake. DC's instructions are quite clear and you should follow them.

Go back to frame 95 and try again.

97 Not quite

You have chosen both the right class number for the main subject and
the right part of the list of general aspects that gives the subdivision
you want, but you have not put them together according to the
instructions. Always read notes and instructions very carefully and
examine the examples.

Now try again
THE ARCHAEOLOGY OF THE PENTATEUCH
221.9302221 turn to frame 106
222.1093 turn to frame 101
222.193 turn to frame 103
222.1022193 turn to frame 110

---

98 No

You have combined the elements of your number the wrong way
round. The subdivision notation cannot stand by itself (or stand first
in a compound number, for that matter) and it must always be added
to a number from the main or auxiliary schedules. The correct
number was
    390.4682 CUSTOMS OF BLACKSMITHS
—682 was the number for BLACKSMITHS in the PERSONS Table.
It must therefore be added to 390.4 CUSTOMS OF PEOPLE OF
VARIOUS SPECIFIC OCCUPATIONS.

Now turn to frame 93

99 No

You have over compensated for your previous mistake. Although you should not *insert* 0 where there is no need, you should leave an 0 in if there is one in the subdivision notation. If you still feel uncertain about the use of the 'Persons' notation from Table 7, go back to frame 94 and read the instruction again.

Otherwise turn to frame 93

---

100 No

For some reason you have omitted the 9 of −918 SLAV RACES when adding the racial, ethnic, national groups notation to the base number 155.84. This is quite wrong. Add *all* of this notation to the number indicated in the schedules.

Now try again
CELTIC FOLK MUSIC
781.72916   turn to frame 94
781.7216   turn to frame 96

In nearly all these cases enough instruction and examples are given in the schedules to make this type of *add* device almost as easy as the first type.

The third type of *add* device is the use of the detailed subdivision of a topic in one subject field for the same or a similar topic when it occurs in another field.

For instance, there is no need to list all the insect pests by name under 632.7 INSECT PESTS, since there is already a list of insects at 595.7 INSECTS in ZOOLOGY, and these may be used to extend 632.7:

> Add to base number 632.7 the numbers following 595.7 in
> 595.71-595.79, eg LOCUSTS 632.726

Another example can be found in 634.9 FORESTRY

> 634.96 INJURIES, DISEASES, PESTS
> Add to base number 634.96 the numbers following 632 in
> 632.1-632.9, eg FOREST FIRES 634.9618

Here the subdivisions of 632 PLANT INJURIES (in this case the original number was 632.18 FROM FIRES) are attached to 634.96

INJURIES, DISEASES [etc]	634.96
FIRES (plant injuries)	632.18
FOREST FIRES	634.9618

Now try this one for yourself
ELECTROPLATING OF COPPER ALLOYS

673.31732   turn to frame 107
673.3732   turn to frame 115
671.73206733   turn to frame 116
673.3   turn to frame 112

The second type of *add* device is used mostly within a class, when its members are all or nearly all divided in the same way. In such a case DC gives a complete list of the subdivisions for one of the members or for the class in general and instructs the classifier to use them and their notation for any other member.

An example can be seen in 617 SURGERY where the subdivisions .01-.09 list general aspects that can be used with any of the particular kinds or applications of surgery listed in 617.1-617.9 that are * starred for an instruction to subdivide.

Another frequently encountered example occurs in HISTORY where each country is supplied with a set of *period subdivisions* which are common to all subdivisions of place within the country, extended by area notation. Thus in 942 GREAT BRITAIN the TUDOR period is given the number 05 so that

TUDOR ENGLAND is	942.05
LANCASHIRE IN THE TUDOR PERIOD is	942.7605
BUCKINGHAMSHIRE UNDER THE TUDORS is	942.5905

Which of these numbers is correct for
THE SYMBOLISM OF THE SONG OF SOLOMON

223.964   turn to frame 97
223.9064   turn to frame 101
220.6402239   turn to frame 106
223.9022064   turn to frame 110

103 No, you have made the same mistake again

Most classes that use this *add* device within their own fields have very clear and specific instructions on where the list of topics can be found that are used as subdivisions and how they are applied. Usually it is a matter of adding a few terminal digits of a general list to the subject subdivisions (ie the ordinary class numbers) in the class with which you are working.

Now go back to frame 102 and read the lesson carefully. Then try the question again.

---

104 No, you have made the same mistake twice

The *add* device, especially in the examples we have seen so far, is really quite simple. The class number you should be using has an instruction to add 001-999 and all you have to do is to add the class number you want for the subject subdivision just as you added area notation when forming a geographical subdivision.

Now go back to frame 91 and read the lesson carefully. Then try the question again.

105 No

You have found the right numbers but you have put them together the wrong way round. This is probably because you did not read the *add* instructions carefully enough, if you read them at all.

In the example A SPECIAL LIBRARY ON NUMISMATICS it is 026 SPECIAL LIBRARIES that says 'Add 001-999 to base number 026 [etc]' and it should be a simple matter to add 737 NUMISMATICS to it to get 026.737.

Now try another
IMPORT DUTIES ON PERFUMES

336.26666854   turn to frame 102
336.26466854   turn to frame 109
668.540336266   turn to frame 104

---

106 No

You have not understood the application of this kind of *add* device. Further you have mistaken what is only the subdivision for the main class and *vice versa*.

In the example THE SYMBOLISM OF THE SONG OF SOLOMON the main subject is THE SONG OF SOLOMON 223.9 and SYMBOLISM is the subdivision. SYMBOLISM is represented for all the books of the BIBLE by the 64 which represents it in DC's general list for the BIBLE: 220.64 SYMBOLISM AND TYPOLOGY. The note in the class number where the subdivisions are to be used always gives clear instructions and examples and these must always be read carefully.

Now try again
COMPLICATIONS OF HEART SURGERY

617.4121   turn to frame 97
617.41201   turn to frame 101
617.010617412   turn to frame 103
617.412061701   turn to frame 110

107 No

You have understood the instruction enough to realise that you must delete the unnecessary digits from the borrowed number, but you must be careful about the application of the rest.

Here you have probably misunderstood the example. However these instructions are phrased, in the type of *add* device we are considering here the application of the borrowed number is largely a matter of taking away the digits which represent the class from which it has been borrowed, leaving only the subdivision.

For instance, in the example FOREST FIRES we are really taking the subdivisions of 632, and so 632, the common element representing the original class, must be ignored.

Now try again
THE STATISTICS OF DEATH FROM PARATYPHOID
312.26   turn to frame 112
312.2669274   turn to frame 111
616.92743122   turn to frame 116
312.269274   turn to frame 115

---

108 No

You have not chosen the correct main class. What you have chosen is the main class originally containing the detailed subdivision. Remember THE MINERALOGY OF SAPPHIRES! You must always ensure that the class number you choose belongs to the correct general subject field.

What you should have done here was to use the subdivision you chose as an extension to the correct main class, where you would have found an instruction telling you to do exactly that.

Now return to frame 115, read the instructions carefully and work the example again.

You have not looked carefully enough at your main class number. The heading (and number) that you have chosen is too general—and in any case there is *no* 'Add 001-999' instruction there!

You should have looked through the schedules of the class a little more carefully, and you would then have found a class reserved especially for this kind of division.

Always check the schedules to see if there is a class more appropriate than the one you first have in mind. Do not forget to use the summary at the beginning of the class if there is one.

SPECIAL LIBRARIES, for example, are given the class 026, to which we may add the number for the subject of the library; this saves any awkward additions to 020. A SPECIAL LIBRARY ON NUMIS-MATICS is therefore 026.737.

Now try
APTITUDE TESTS FOR MATHEMATICAL ABILITY
153.951   turn to frame 104
153.9451   turn to frame 102
510.15394 turn to frame 105

You have realised (quite correctly) that you must add to the class number a subdivision borrowed from the model list, but you have not realised that since this operates within the class there is no need to repeat the digits that reveal the borrowed number's origin.

In the example THE SYMBOLISM OF THE SONG OF SOLOMON only 64 needs to be taken from 220.64 SYMBOLISM OF THE BIBLE —the 22 represents the BIBLE of which THE SONG OF SOLOMON is a part. The correct answer for this reason is not 223.90220964 but 223.9064.

Try this one
WEAVING COTTON

677.2106702824   turn to frame 103
677.212824   turn to frame 97
677.2124   turn to frame 101
677.0282406721   turn to frame 106

---

111 No. You have made the same mistake twice

This kind of *add* device is quite easy to use. All you have to do is to use the terminal or variable digits of the class number which supplies your subdivision. The constant digits of that original class are not needed and should be ignored.

Now go back to frame 101 and read the lesson carefully. Then try the question again.

You have not followed the *add* instruction.

This class is one which may be extended in detail by the application of subdivisions from another class. There are too many of these in the scheme for DC to itemise subdivisions every time, and this, as we have seen, is one way of keeping the printed scheme a manageable size.

There is no difficulty about the application of this kind of subdivision, if you remember the method we followed with the geographical subdivision built into one class number.

In the example FOREST FIRES the instruction at 634.96 INJURIES [etc] says

> Add to base number 634.96 the numbers following 632 in
> 632.1-632.9, eg FOREST FIRES 634.9618

All you have to do is to compare this with the borrowed number for PLANT INJURIES FROM FIRES 632.18. It is very easy to see from this that 632 has been ignored and only the 18 representing the subdivision FIRES has been added to the class concerned: 634.96 INJURIES [etc].

Try this one
THE WURTZ-FITTIG REACTION AS AN INDUSTRIAL CHEMICAL PROCESS

660.2844   turn to frame 111
660.284421   turn to frame 107
660.28441   turn to frame 115
547.21660284   turn to frame 116

113 No, you are wrong

You have observed that at the general level, DC lists standard subdivisions as .001 etc, with the particular instruction
.008-.009 standard subdivisions
Notations from Table 1
and you have continued to use the double zero even for subdivisions of 658. This is wrong. DC uses the double zero at the general level to allow a distinction between a special subdivision like
658.023 MANAGEMENT OF LARGE SCALE ENTERPRISES
and a general or standard subdivision like
658.0023 THE PROFESSION OR OCCUPATION OF
MANAGEMENT
However, DC assumes that once any special subdivision has been used there is no need for any further notational distinction. With
658.023 MANAGEMENT OF LARGE SCALE ENTERPRISES
a further 023 could mean *only* PROFESSION OR OCCUPATION and so a double zero is unnecessary.
Occasionally, DC does persist in using the double zero for special reasons—look, for example, at 617 SURGERY AND RELATED TOPICS.

Now try again
AN ENCYCLOPEDIA OF PATHOLOGY

616.0703   turn to frame 121
616.07003   turn to frame 120

---

114 No. You have made the same mistake twice   .

Although this kind of *add* device looks complex it is really no different from the kinds you have met already. All you need to do is to match the last digits of the main number you are using with the last digits of the borrowed number and see at what point you must begin to use them.

Now return to frame 115 and read the lesson carefully. Then try the question again.

A more complex form of this kind of *add* device occurs when not one but several subdivisions are reserved for extension by subdivisions from another class. The borrowed subdivisions are important so more than just one place of the borrowing class is made available to receive them. Again, the notation is shorter, but the application a little less easy to understand.

What DC does is to give a *base number* (we met this when dealing with area notation) derived from the range of notation in the class you are concerned with, and to include it in the usual kind of *add* instruction.

For example the naming of SPECIFIC FLOWERS in 635.9 FLORI-CULTURE is made possible by the reservation of the subclasses 635.933-.939 for parallel subdivision like 583-589. This might seem complicated were it not for DC's instruction:

Add to base number 635.93, the numbers following 58 in
583-589, eg CACTUS 635.93347

In other words, since the final digits 3-9 of 635.933-.939 are already present in 583-589, DC derives the base number 635.93 for a normal *add* device.

635.933-.939   FLOWERS BY FAMILY [etc]
635.93   [base number]
  583-589   FLOWERS (botany)
  583.47   CACTUS (botany)
635.93347   CACTUS (floriculture)

What is the number for
DYEING WILD SILK
667.392   turn to frame 119
667.3392   turn to frame 117
677.392   turn to frame 108
667.31392 turn to frame 122

You have found the original class number for the specific subject and you have added to it the class number for the general field you are really concerned with. They are the wrong way round.

Always make sure that the class number you choose belongs to the correct subject field. (Remember THE MINERALOGY OF SAPPHIRES.)

If you had read the schedules carefully at the correct class you would have seen an instruction telling you to add the detailed subdivision from the class where it is originally listed.

In the example FOREST FIRES the instruction at 634.96 INJURIES [etc] says

> Add to base number 634.96 the numbers following 632 in
> 632.1-632.9, eg FOREST FIRES 634.9618

All you have to do is to compare 634.9618 with the borrowed number for PLANT INJURIES FROM FIRES 632.18. It is easy to see from this that 632 has been ignored and only the 18 representing the subdivision FIRES has been added to the class concerned: 634.96 INJURIES [etc].

Now try another
ANTHROPOMETRIC STUDIES OF THE HUMERUS

573.6   turn to frame 112
573.6717   turn to frame 115
611.71705736   turn to frame 111
573.611717   turn to frame 107

The form of *add* device that you have just learned about is not difficult if you proceed slowly and think clearly. With it you have mastered the most complex form of the addition of single subdivisions that DC uses.

Sometimes it is necessary to use synthesis twice or even three times in the same class number. Generally speaking unless a note in the schedules invites you to do this it is better to limit synthesis to one addition, but there are some classes whose subject naturally requires more, and some occasions when almost any subject may need more. We can divide multiple synthesis roughly into several kinds and we shall look at these one by one. They include:

The use of a standard subdivision after some other subdivision like an *add* device or area notation;

The use of physiographic features from Table 2: Areas with other area notations;

The use of two added subdivisions in a subject for the sake of difference or comparison;

The use of general aspects of a subject with other constructed divisions of that subject.

Remember, however, that except in cases involving tables of subdivision that can be used anywhere in DC, you should beware of trying too hard to link up subdivisions from the schedules unless DC instructs or permits you to do so.

Now turn to frame 118 and continue.

118 Very often you will want to add a standard subdivision to a class number in which you have already used another kind of subdivision.

Look at 391 COSTUME in the schedules. You will see there that, as we have noticed with other classes previously, DC instructs you to use 391.001-.007 for the standard subdivisions. This is because DC uses the subdivisions 391.01-.05 for COSTUMES OF SPECIFIC CLASSES OF PEOPLE with an *add* instruction for the detail. Clearly we could not then use 391.01-.05 for standard subdivisions or we should be using 391.022 for both ILLUSTRATIONS OF COSTUME (standard subdivision 022 means ILLUSTRATIONS) and COSTUMES OF ROYALTY. DC tells us therefore to use a *double* zero for standard subdivision, which serves to distinguish the two subjects.

391.022 COSTUMES OF ROYALTY

391.0022 ILLUSTRATIONS OF COSTUME

This much we have learned already. What we need now is a way of using both *special* and *general* subdivisions together—to be able to say, for example, ILLUSTRATIONS OF COSTUMES OF ROYALTY.

In spite of the appearance of the instruction at 391 (and this is true of all such instructions) you do *not* have to use a double zero for standard subdivision within the class. Once 022 ROYALTY has been added to 391 there is no likelihood of mistaking a further *single* zero for anything but a standard subdivision. ILLUSTRATIONS can thus remain 022, to make 391.022022 ILLUSTRATIONS OF COSTUMES OF ROYALTY. The first 022 *must* mean ROYALTY according to the schedules, and the second (once the first kind of subdivision has been used) must be a standard subdivision.

Instructions to use *double* zeros apply *only* to the class numbers where they are given and *not* to any of their subdivisions. DC has worked out the effect of this and you are quite safe to use the standard subdivisions in the normal way. In any case where there might be confusion DC has an instruction telling you what to do and a list of the kinds of subdivision and how to apply them.

Now try one yourself
THE MANAGEMENT OF LARGE SCALE ENTERPRISES IN GERMANY

658.02300943 turn to frame 113
658.0230943   turn to frame 121

119 No

You have contracted the borrowed number too far. You should always study the example given in the instruction very carefully, and compare it with the original class number from which the borrowed subdivision has been taken.

RUSSIAN SHORTHAND

653.49171   turn to frame 117
653.499171   turn to frame 122
653.4171   turn to frame 114
491.71   turn to frame 108

---

120 No, you are still making the same mistake

A double zero is needed only for standard subdivisions of the heading because that heading also has special subdivisions that are introduced by a single zero, like 617.07 PATHOLOGY. If standard subdivisions were not given an extra zero then PATHOLOGY would be confused at 617.07 with STUDY AND TEACHING OF SURGERY. But at any of the special subdivisions themselves there is no further subdivision that uses a zero other than a standard subdivision, so the normal practice can be adopted.

Now go back to frame 118 and read the explanation carefully. Then try the question again.

Another kind of double synthesis involves specifying both the place and the period of a subject. Earlier in the programme you used period divisions by themselves with simple class numbers. Quite often, however, you will have to use period divisions after you have used area notation, to specify time as well as place. This is quite easily done. Period divisions for each region or country are given in the HISTORY classes 930-990. In those classes the instructions for further subdivision include

01-09 Historical periods

within each country, whose detail is provided from Table 2: AREAS.

Thus, any geographical subdivision within a subject may be augmented by period subdivision in the same way. For example, in 946 HISTORY OF SPAIN the period subdivision for the MOORISH DYNASTIES is 02, so we may add this to the area notation -46 SPAIN as a general time-and-place subdivision for any subject to mean IN SPAIN UNDER THE MOORISH DYNASTIES.

Try one for yourself
RUSSIAN SCIENCE UNDER STALIN

509.4709042   turn to frame 129
509.470842   turn to frame 125
509.47090842   turn to frame 132

It is important always to study the example given in the *add* instruction in order to avoid including too many digits from the borrowed number (as you have done here) or removing too many. You should compare the example given in the instruction with the original class number from which the borrowed subdivision has been taken.

Now try again
AUTOMATION IN THE ELECTRONICS INDUSTRY

621.38   turn to frame 108
338.4562138   turn to frame 117
338.45662138 turn to frame 114
338.45638   turn to frame 119

123 No. You have just made the same mistake twice

This addition of a period subdivision to area notation is quite simple
if you remember to take it from the country's own schedules in the
main class HISTORY, and to add it using a single zero as an indicator.

Now turn back to frame 121 and read the explanation again carefully
and the instruction in DC at −3-9 SPECIFIC CONTINENTS,
COUNTRIES [etc]. Then try the question again.

---

124 No, you are still making the same mistake

Return to frame 125 and read the instruction again. Follow DC's
instructions when you work the problem and see if you can get the
right answer this time.

Time and place are not the only kinds of subdivision that may be used together. It is possible sometimes to join RACIAL, ETHNIC, NATIONAL GROUPS and AREAS; or PERSONS and AREAS.

For example, 305 SOCIAL STRUCTURE contains 305.8 RACIAL, ETHNIC, NATIONAL GROUPS which says

> Add 'Racial, Ethnic, National Groups' notation 01-99 from Table 5 to base number 305.8, eg CHINESE 305.8951; then, unless it is redundant, add 0 and to the result add 'Areas' notation 1-9 from Table 2, eg CHINESE IN THE UNITED STATES 305.8951073

Note the use of the 0 to separate and signal the second subdivision.

What is the number for
EDUCATION OF GYPSIES IN GREAT BRITAIN

371.9791497041 turn to frame 135
371.9741091497 turn to frame 130
371.979149741   turn to frame 133

126 No, you are wrong

You are still making the same mistake. It is very simple to use the special Table of subdivisions. To the starred class number (or to the base number that DC gives you in doubtful cases) add the notation from Table 4.

Now go to 128, read the instruction again, and try the problem once more.

---

127 No

The 'Areas' notation is correct in both cases, but you have combined the elements in the wrong order. DC specifically instructs you to put the country emphasised first, and the other country second. If in doubt you should in any case use the *earlier* notation first. Always follow DC's instructions.

Now turn to frame 128.

128 Two classes have special Tables of subdivision of their own. At one time these classes were fully enumerated, and had quite elaborate instructions to add sections of notation from one subclass to numbers in another subclass. But now they have been tidied up, and you may use the special subdivisions just as you have become used to using the general subdivisions like persons or areas or forms of presentation.

First look at the table for 400 LANGUAGE. It is Table 4: SUBDIVISIONS OF INDIVIDUAL LANGUAGES, listing problems, aspects, tools etc. This notation may be added to any starred item in 400 LANGUAGE—though not of course to a starred item in any other class. Thus PORTUGUESE GRAMMAR combines 469 PORTUGUESE and −5 STRUCTURAL SYSTEM (GRAMMAR) from the special Table of subdivisions, to make 469.5.

What is
A DICTIONARY OF STANDARD CZECHOSLOVAKIAN

491.863   turn to frame 144
491.8603   turn to frame 136
491.86   turn to frame 141

129 No

You are trying to use a number from the *general* historical periods given in the standard subdivisions. These can be used only when no country or locality is specified. If a country or locality is specified then period subdivisions must be taken from that country's schedules in the HISTORY main class, and added to the area notation with a single zero as indicator, as it is in nearly all countries.

Now try again
POSTAL COMMUNICATION IN EIGHTEENTH CENTURY EUROPE

383.4940253   turn to frame 125
383.494090253   turn to frame 132
383.49409033   turn to frame 123

---

130 No, you are wrong

You have put the 'Areas' notation *before* the 'Racial, Ethnic, National Groups' notation; DC tells you to do just the opposite. If your answer meant anything at all (and it doesn't) it might mean something like THE EDUCATION OF BRITONS IN GYPSY ENCAMPMENTS.

Try another example, and this time follow DC's instructions carefully.
THE SOCIAL STRUCTURE OF ITALIANS IN QUEBEC

305.8714051   turn to frame 124
305.8510714   turn to frame 135

131 You are quite right

Very occasionally you may find yourself using quite sophisticated combinations of notation. If for instance you wanted to find a number for THE EDUCATION OF IRAQI STUDENTS IN ENGLISH SPEAK-ING COUNTRIES you begin with 371.97 to which you add (as DC instructs) 927 for ARAB AND MALTESE, further divided by 'Area' notation 567 for IRAQ. After the separating 0 you add 175 REGIONS WHERE SPECIFIC LANGUAGES PREDOMINATE, extended by 'Languages' notation 21 for ENGLISH. The assembled number is thus
        371.97927567017521

You probably think this is far too complex and cumbersome a notation to use. And you would be right. It is very rare either to find a book on such a complex subject; special collections may include such documents, but you would probably not then use DC anyway. More-over it is rare to find DC permitting such clumsy notation. As we shall see in a moment, DC prefers simplicity if possible and instructs you accordingly. We included this example just to show what can some-times be done with the Tables of subdivisions.

Now turn to frame 128

---

132 No

You are using the correct historical period number, taken from the schedules for the country in the main class HISTORY, but you have tried to use it in the same way that you used the *general* historical periods from the standard subdivisions. Those are for use only when no country or locality is specified and are not relevant at all here. When you use a period subdivision from a country's historical schedules all you have to do is to use a single zero as an indicator, as happens in most countries' historical schedules.

Now try again
DAMS AND RESERVOIRS IN REPUBLICAN ROME

627.80937602   turn to frame 125
627.8093760902   turn to frame 129
627.80937609014   turn to frame 129

133 No, that is the wrong number

You have followed DC's instructions quite properly in putting the
'Racial, Ethnic, National Groups' notation first, and the place second,
but you omitted the 0 that DC uses as a separator and indicator.

Try another one
THE SOCIAL STRUCTURE OF ITALIANS IN QUEBEC
305.851714   turn to frame 124
305.8510714   turn to frame 135

---

134 No, this is the wrong answer

You have chosen a perfectly good number for PLOT IN SPANISH
FICTION, but you have ignored the form and the period—both of them
probably of greater significance. DC's instruction is first to choose the
subdivision of *greatest significance* (the subdivision with fewest zeroes)
and then to see if it may be subdivided further.

Now go to frame 153 and try again.

Of course it is also possible in certain circumstances to combine two subdivisions of *the same kind* and DC will always give you appropriate instructions. As we have just seen with the combination of RACIAL, ETHNIC, NATIONAL GROUPS and AREAS notations, a zero is used to separate and distinguish the second subdivision.

For example, in 341 INTERNATIONAL LAW, the subclass 341.0266 BILATERAL TREATIES needs dividing by both countries involved in the treaty. A TREATY BETWEEN THE UNITED STATES AND BRAZIL is shown as

    341.0266   BILATERAL TREATIES
    341.026673   BILATERAL TREATIES OF THE US
    341.026673081 BILATERAL TREATIES OF THE US AND BRAZIL

The two Area codes are used in notational order, though DC does offer an alternative: to give priority to the country requiring local emphasis. In the example shown here, a *Brazilian* library might place BRAZIL first: 341.026681073.

Find the correct number for
FOREIGN RELATIONS BETWEEN FRANCE AND CAMBODIA
327.440596   turn to frame 131
327.596044   turn to frame 127

136 No

You have assumed that the special subdivision notation needs a 0 to
indicate its presence. This is not necessary, and indeed is contrary to
the instructions in DC. The notation from Table 4 is to be added
directly to the base number. Remember the example of PORTUGUESE
GRAMMAR, that combined 469 and −5 to make 469.5.

Now try again
PRONUNCIATION OF UKRAINIAN
491.79152   turn to frame 144
491.79   turn to frame 141
491.790152   turn to frame 126

---

137 No

You have combined the numbers in the wrong order.
DC's general instruction on combining language numbers to describe
bilingual dictionaries is to use the less known language number first,
because dictionaries are customarily sought to translate from the less
known languages. If you are in doubt as to which is the less known
language, then you should use first the notation that comes *later* in the
schedules. Of course you may have good reasons, depending on your
users or your stock, to vary that order. But here we have a normal
situation, without special circumstances. So you should put the later
number first, and then add the earlier number after the 3 that means
DICTIONARIES.

Now try
A RUSSIAN/TURKISH DICTIONARY
491.739435   turn to frame 140
494.3539171   turn to frame 146

138   No, you have chosen the wrong number

Although it is true that 820 is ENGLISH LITERATURE, and that
−08003 is correct notation for the ELIZABETHAN PERIOD, formed
from −080 base number in Table 3, with an additional 0 as instructed
in Table 3-A, followed by −3 ELIZABETHAN in the period table for
ENGLISH LITERATURE, you did not notice that 82 is the base
number for ENGLISH LITERATURE—*not* 820. The correct answer
should have been
> 820.8003 A COLLECTION OF ELIZABETHAN ENGLISH
> LITERATURE

Try another one
A COLLECTION OF EARLY MEDIEVAL GERMAN LITERATURE
830.08001   turn to frame 148
830.8001   turn to frame 142

---

139   No

You are making the mistake (which you have probably made before)
of ignoring the base number that DC gives you in any class whose
notation is not appropriate for the addition of a subdivision, so that
your resulting number has too many zeroes.

Try again
A COLLECTION OF FRENCH LANGUAGE LITERATURE BY
WRITERS OF THE AFRO-ASIAN BLOC
840.80917165   turn to frame 152
840.080917165   turn to frame 145
840.809017165   turn to frame 149

140 No

You are still making the same mistake. In situations where no particular
interest is involved, the base number is the one for the *less known*
language, or the one whose class number occurs *later* in the schedule.
In this case the answer should have been
     494.3539171 A RUSSIAN/TURKISH DICTIONARY
because 494.35 TURKISH occurs later in the schedules than 491.7.

Now go to frame 144 and try again.

---

141 No

You have not added the notation from the subdivision at all. It is true
that some numbers in 400 LANGUAGE cannot be extended by subdivision notation, but all of the starred places may be—and this was one
of the starred places.

Try another one
ETYMOLOGY OF BRETON
491.68   turn to frame 126
491.6802   turn to frame 136
491.682   turn to frame 144

Further detail for -08 COLLECTIONS and -09 HISTORY, listing
features, elements, themes, and author/reader characteristics, is taken
from Table 3-A, which follows immediately. For example 09 HISTORY,
DESCRIPTION, CRITICAL APPRAISAL in Table 3 includes

-091-099 LITERATURE DISPLAYING SPECIFIC FEATURES
OR EMPHASISING SUBJECT VALUES, AND FOR
AND BY SPECIFIC KINDS OF PERSONS
Add to -09 notations 1-9 from Table 3-A, eg HISTORY
AND DESCRIPTION OF LITERATURE ON FAUST
-09351

Thus the Table 3-A notation 13 for IDEALISM may be added to
-09 to make a general literature subdivision 0913 IDEALISM. This in
turn allows the normal construction 840.913 IDEALISM IN FRENCH
LITERATURE.

Some notations in Table 3-A may be further extended by adding
notation from appropriate tables, eg 8 LITERATURE FOR AND BY
VARIOUS SPECIFIC RACIAL, ETHNIC, NATIONAL GROUPS, which
has the instruction

Add 'Racial, Ethnic, National Groups' notation 03-99 from
Table 5 to 8, eg LITERATURE BY AFRICANS AND PERSONS
OF AFRICAN DESCENT 896 [where 96 is AFRICANS etc]

So 820 ENGLISH LITERATURE (base number 82) may be extended by
098 HISTORY OF LITERATURES BY SPECIAL GROUPS which may
be further extended by -96 AFRICANS [etc] from Table 5, to make

820.9896 A HISTORY OF ENGLISH LANGUAGE LITERA-
TURE BY AFRICANS AND PERSONS OF AFRICAN
DESCENT

Now find a number for
A COLLECTION OF GERMAN LANGUAGE LITERATURE BY
ENGINEERS
830.809262   turn to frame 152
830.0809262   turn to frame 139
830.80920962 turn to frame 149

143 No, you are wrong

You have chosen a perfectly good number for SEVENTEENTH CEN-
TURY SPANISH FICTION but you have ignored both NOVELLAS
and PLOT. It could be that either or both may be used to extend
863.3 to be nearer what you want.

Go to frame 153 and try again.

---

144 Good

You probably noticed the instruction under —3 DICTIONARIES (etc)
in Table 4; it offers a way to deal with BILINGUAL DICTIONARIES
that is very useful, and of course frequently necessary. It is a synthesis
similar to the synthesis you have already met in combining notations
from the other tables of subdivisions.

SANSKRIT is 491.2; a SANSKRIT DICTIONARY is 491.23; a
SANSKRIT/ENGLISH DICTIONARY adds —21 from Table 6: LAN-
GUAGES to make 491.2321.

It is usual to make the less familiar language the main number (since
it is the less familiar language we probably want to translate)—but if
there is any doubt we should use the language number that occurs *later*
in the schedules as the main number.

Now try one for yourself
A BULGARIAN/FRENCH DICTIONARY
491.81341 turn to frame 146
443.9181   turn to frame 137

145 No, you are wrong

You have made the same mistake twice, through not reading DC's instructions properly. The addition of subdivision notation is simple if you follow the instructions and read the examples carefully as you go.

Go back to frame 142 and read the explanation again carefully. Then try the problem once more.

---

146 Good

Another class that has its own special table of subdivisions is 800 LITERATURE: Table 3 SUBDIVISIONS OF INDIVIDUAL LITERA-TURES. At one time DC had many *add* instructions in this class and you would have had to consult the schedules in several places to find all the pieces of notation that might make up even as apparently simple a subject as REALISM IN FRENCH CLASSICAL DRAMA.

Now, however, the use of Table 3 for the 800 class makes it very easy. Remember that Table 3 may be used only with class 800, and never with any other, and its notation must be used with a starred number from the schedules—never alone. Note that in many cases (particularly of the major literatures) DC has carefully shown you the *base number* to use when adding notation from the special table.

The main part of the table is a complete list of features, forms and periods of literature, in various combinations; the last part is a brief indication of how to arrange criticism, biography and the works of single authors. We are concerned here with the first part.

Have a look at the schedules at 840 LITERATURES OF ROMANCE LANGUAGES. FRENCH LITERATURE, and note that DC shows 84 as the base number. Then look for the table of subdivision so that you will be able to use it in the next few frames.

Now turn to frame 147

147   800 LITERATURE has a rather more complex table of subdivisions—Table 3: SUBDIVISIONS OF INDIVIDUAL LITERATURES. First of all remember that each INDIVIDUAL LITERATURE listed in the 800 class displays only its period subdivisions, a *general* list of the forms of literature (repeated and supplemented in Table 3), and any special subdivisions for regional or dialect literature, including any periods of development peculiar to them.

At the beginning of Table 3 there is a two page explanation of the use of Tables 3 and 3-A; in essence it is that the order of assembling subdivisions is form of literature/period/form of document (eg collection, critical work, etc), *except that* if the *form* of literature extends below the single level of poetry, drama, etc, eg LYRIC poetry, then the periods may *not* be specified.

Table 3 includes several kinds of subdivision. The first is simply the *standard subdivisions* from Table 1 to be applied to any individual literature, eg 869 PORTUGUESE LITERATURE extended by -03 ENCYCLOPEDIA to make 869.03 AN ENCYCLOPEDIA OF PORTUGUESE LITERATURE. The second is the modified *standard subdivisions* -08 COLLECTIONS and -09 HISTORY; they have special significance in LITERATURE and their detail is laid out explicitly in Table 3. -08 and -09 may be further divided first of all by period notation *taken from the INDIVIDUAL LITERATURES in 800* and added to -08 or -09 after a *double zero*, eg 869.09003 PORTUGUESE LITERATURE:HISTORY:19TH CENTURY. Note that DC is slightly confusing in its explanation of the application of period subdivision in -08 and -09. But in spite of the different instructions, double zero subdivision is the result.

What is the number for
A COLLECTION OF ELIZABETHAN LITERATURE

820.08003   turn to frame 138
820.8003   turn to frame 142

148 No

You have made the same mistake twice. As with the standard subdivisions that you met earlier in this book you should eliminate unnecessary zeroes. Actually DC makes this easy for you, by telling you in 830
GERMAN LITERATURE that the base number to which you add subdivision notation is 83. This means that 83 and 08001 become 830.8001,
because the decimal point always occurs after the third digit.

Now go back to frame 147 and try again.

---

149 No, you are wrong

You have too many zeroes. Although you found -08 COLLECTIONS
and added to the base number -080 the number 9 LITERATURE FOR
AND BY SPECIFIC KINDS OF PERSON, which includes 93-99 FOR
AND BY PERSONS RESIDENT IN SPECIFIC CONTINENTS,
COUNTRIES, LOCALITIES, still you have added the extension to
that notation *after another zero*. There is no need to do this, and in any
case DC instructs you specifically to add further notation directly.

Try again
A COLLECTION OF SPANISH LANGUAGE LITERATURE BY
GERMANS

860.80943   turn to frame 152
860.080943   turn to frame 139
860.809043   turn to frame 145

150 The major part of each of these subdivisions of literary form is division by period, using the appropriate notation from the period table of the literature you are concerned with. For example in −1 POETRY, −11-19 SPECIFIC PERIODS says

> Add to −1 the notation from the period table for the specific literature [etc]

So to 82 (base number) ENGLISH LITERATURE we add −1 POETRY (base number for period division) and 3 ELIZABETHAN PERIOD, to make

821.3 ELIZABETHAN POETRY

Before we go any further try one for yourself
SPANISH DRAMA OF THE GOLDEN AGE
862.3   turn to frame 153
862.13   turn to frame 164

---

151 No

You have ignored the order of precedence specified by DC. This order has been worked out so that you can place a compound subject in the most useful place. You have chosen what seems to you the most likely place, but it is not what DC wants you to do.

Now try another
THE PSYCHOLOGY OF FOSTER CHILDREN OF PRE-SCHOOL AGE
155.445 turn to frame 161
155.423 turn to frame 160

Now look at the rest of Table 3: SUBDIVISIONS OF INDIVIDUAL
LITERATURES. From here on (-1-8) it is concerned chiefly with the
forms of literature, —1 POETRY, —2 DRAMA, etc, to make

821   ENGLISH POETRY

895.11 CHINESE POETRY

Like -08 and -09, each subdivision may be divided by *features,
elements, themes* taken from Table 3-A.

Many of the literary form subdivisions -1-8 may also be divided into
specific kinds, eg -102 DRAMATIC POETRY, -103 EPIC POETRY,
-106 DESCRIPTIVE [etc] to make

821.02 ENGLISH DRAMATIC POETRY

Indeed, many of these forms may be subdivided by Table 3-A as
instructed by the footnote in Table 3:

*Add as instructed under -1-8

so that ROMANTICISM IN ENGLISH DRAMATIC POETRY extends
821.02 by subdivisions of -1-8 that include -09 HISTORY, DESCRIP-
TION, CRITICAL APPRAISAL further subdivided by notations from
Table 3-A that include -145 ROMANTICISM. The final number is

821.0209145 ROMANTICISM IN ENGLISH DRAMATIC
POETRY

Now turn to frame 150

Unlike the other subdivision notations we have seen so far, the period subdivisions in literature may sometimes be subdivided further, by the addition of notation for *features, elements, themes* (etc) from Table 3, or from Table 3-A, added to -08 or -09. For example we have already met -09145 ROMANTICISM, when we made up the number

821.0209145 ROMANTICISM IN ENGLISH DRAMATIC
POETRY

So we can also express ROMANTICISM IN ELIZABETHAN POETRY by adding 09145 to 821.3 ELIZABETHAN POETRY to make

821.309145 ROMANTICISM IN ELIZABETHAN POETRY

Note, however, that you combine notation in this way only for collections and general works of criticism; *single* authors may not be treated in this way, but may either have everything by and about them collected together in the appropriate period, or simply at the appropriate form.

What is the correct number for
PLOT IN SEVENTEENTH CENTURY SPANISH NOVELLAS

863.00924   turn to frame 134
863.3   turn to frame 143
863.30924   turn to frame 158

154 No

You have ignored the order of precedence specified by DC. This order has been worked out so that you can place a compound subject in the most useful place. You have chosen what seems to you the most likely place, but it is not what DC wants you to do.

Now try another
THE PSYCHOLOGY OF FOSTER CHILDREN OF PRE-SCHOOL AGE

155.445   turn to frame 161
155.423   turn to frame 160

---

155 No, you have the wrong answer

You did not read DC's instructions carefully enough and you are becoming confused. This time you have chosen to have too *few* 1's. 839.31 is DUTCH LITERATURE, so 839.311 is DUTCH POETRY. We know already that −1 divides directly by period, so that RENAISSANCE DUTCH POETRY must be 839.3112.

Now go back to frame 150, read the explanation again carefully and work the problem once more.

156 No

A centred heading cannot provide you with a class number, since by
its nature it covers several, but not all, of the ten subdivisions available
to a class. DC does not allow you to say, for example 669.1-669.7,
since this would be awkward to file. Instead you must use the next
higher single number—in this case 669.

Now try
AIRCRAFT
623.741-623.746 turn to frame 167
623.74   turn to frame 163
623.741   turn to frame 159

---

157 No

You have made a valiant attempt at synthesis, but you have gone too far.
You have assembled all the elements in what is theoretically the right
order, and in what might be the right way. But DC does not want you
to do this, in the interests of a simple, easily understood notation. So
the instruction tells you to use period subdivision, and further divide
that by literary feature—*and that is all.*

Now go back to 153 and try another answer.

The need to choose between different features or aspects of a compound subject is well illustrated in 800 LITERATURE, where quite specific instruction is given. We have seen already in other classes that sometimes DC offers different kinds of division of the class that theoretically could appear in combination, but that DC wishes to be used singly. In cases of this kind DC usually gives a table of precedence or priorities. For example, in 155.4-.6 PSYCHOLOGY OF SPECIFIC AGES AND SEXES, 155.42-155.45 includes SPECIFIC GROUPINGS. MALE INFANT TWINS could be placed variously at

    155.422 INFANTS
    155.432 BOYS
    155.444 TWINS

but DC's precedence table compels us to use 155.444 TWINS. Sometimes DC replaces a table of precedence by a simple instruction to choose the earlier or earliest notation; and sometimes to choose the later or last notation.

Now choose a number for
FEMALE MIGRANT WORKERS AGED 16-18

331.544   turn to frame 154
331.34   turn to frame 161
331.4   turn to frame 151

159 No

You have chosen a heading which is only a part of the subject you should have in mind. A centred heading covers several subdivisions and is thus not a class number in itself; if you have a subject that can be described by the centred heading then you must use the next higher single class number.

Now try again
PORCELAIN

738.27-738.28   turn to frame 156
738.2   turn to frame 163
738.27   turn to frame 167

---

160 No

You are still not using the order of precedence correctly.

This is not different fundamentally from the many instructions that you see in DC that tell you to class operations on specific objects with the objects, and to ignore the operations.

Now go back to frame 158 and read the lesson again. Then try the question again, keeping the explanation and examples in mind.

A new and most important table of precedence appears on page 1 of
volume 1, to help you choose among standard subdivisions. That is,
if a document might be described as ILLUSTRATION (-028) of the
TECHNIQUE (-022) of a subject, then -028 should be chosen over
-022. The order of precedence may not seem at first to be particularly
logical: PHILOSOPHY (a form) precedes PLACE which is then suc-
ceeded by PROGRAMMED TEXTS (a different kind of form).
Actually the list does reflect an amalgam of Sayers' ideas of inner
and outer form and Ranganathan's fundamental categories, albeit
overlaid in an unusual way. However, the classifier must consult the
table carefully whenever two kinds of standard subdivision may occur.

Sometimes a DC class or list has no table of precedence. In that
case you should consider choosing the specific notation that stands
latest in the schedules. This is because a classification schedule reflects
shelf order and thus usually proceeds from general to specific; of
course you should check the order within the class in case this is not
true, but it is often a good guide.

For example in the special Table 3-A of literature subdivisions
there is no table of precedence to tell you how to handle a subject like
ROMANTICISM IN LITERATURE BY AFRICANS. But since
ROMANTICISM has the notation 145 in Table 3-A and LITERATURE
FOR AND BY VARIOUS RACIAL, ETHNIC, NATIONAL GROUPS
has the notation 8 (extended in this case for AFRICANS to 896) it is
896 that must be added to the base number of the INDIVIDUAL
LITERATURE.

Now turn to frame 165

You have chosen a perfectly good number for SPANISH NOVELLAS,
but you have ignored both period and literary problems—and either
might be used to extend the number you have chosen, and thus be a
better description of PLOT IN SEVENTEENTH CENTURY SPANISH
NOVELLAS.

Go back to frame 153 and try once more.

163 Good, you are right

Sometimes DC does not wish you to use the next higher single class number for an area covered by a centred heading and then you will find an instruction telling you what to do. For example, the centred heading 250-280 CHRISTIAN CHURCH instructs you to use 260 for comprehensive works, rather than 250. Take care always to read the notes and instructions to see if they help you in this way.

Now try
THE INSTRUMENTS OF THE STRING QUARTET

787.1-787.4	turn to frame 156
787.01	turn to frame 168
787.1	turn to frame 159
787	turn to frame 166

---

164 No, you are being careless

It is true that we used a −1 to introduce PERIODS in our example, but that was because −1 meant POETRY, for 821.3 ELIZABETHAN POETRY. In SPANISH DRAMA, the −2 means DRAMA, and it is subdivided directly by PERIOD, just like −1. So the correct answer is
     862.3 SPANISH DRAMA OF THE GOLDEN AGE

Try another one
DUTCH RENAISSANCE POETRY

839.3112	turn to frame 153
839.312	turn to frame 155

165 The choice among different kinds of subdivision is symptomatic of DC's practical approach to classification and the provision of easily recognised and used labels for the subjects of books and the books themselves. Another feature of this kind in DC is the centred heading now used to give specific mention of general topics covering some, but not all, of the subdivisions of a general class.

Centred headings are particularly useful when a level of division would not normally be revealed by the addition of another digit in the class number, as when only a few of the ten places available for subdivision are used and the rest used for another principle of division.

For example, in 616.9 DISEASES—OTHER DISEASES, 616.91-616.96 are given over to COMMUNICABLE DISEASES, and 616.97-616.99 are used for other topics, like 616.97 ALLERGIES AND AUTOIMMUNE DISEASES. 616.91-616.96 is therefore made a *centred heading* with the characteristic black stylized arrow in the left margin.

▶ 616.91-616.96 COMMUNICABLE DISEASES

Clearly a centred heading cannot give you a class number; by its nature it covers a group of numbers and serves only to define a subject area in the schedules. If the book you have to classify covers only one or two of the headings contained in the centred heading then you should use the first of the subordinate class numbers. But if the book you have to classify covers three or more of the headings contained in the centred heading then you must put it at the next higher single number.

In our example of 616 DISEASES a book on COMMUNICABLE DISEASES (centred heading 616.91-616.96) would take the class number 616.9; but a book on ERUPTIVE DISEASES would take the number 616.91.

Now try this for yourself
EXTRACTIVE METALLURGY OF FERROUS AND NON-FERROUS METALS

669.1   turn to frame 159
669   turn to frame 163
669.1-669.7   turn to frame 156

166 No. You have done precisely what you were warned not to do

787.1-787.4 has an instruction to use 787.01 for **BOWED INSTRU-MENTS IN GENERAL**, rather than the general number 787.

Remember that DC always has an instruction telling you what number you should use instead of the range of notation at the centred heading.

Now go on to frame 168

---

167 No, you have just made the same mistake again

Centred headings were an innovation in DC17, but they do no more than rationalise a general principle. You have always had to use a more general number for a wide range of subordinate topics for which there is no single class number, and that is precisely what you are being asked to do here.

Now go back to frame 165 and read the lesson carefully. Then try the question again.

168 You have now worked through most of the kinds of problems that using DC might present. Always remember that the schedules give very clear examples and instructions, and in addition you will often find subjects in the index that appear in the schedules only in scope notes, or even that do not appear at all, but are the results of synthesis. In very difficult cases you may derive some extra help from your knowledge of classification theory, as you will see.

We learned very early that we could not always expect to find places in the classification scheme exactly equal to the subjects we were trying to classify. Indeed it was to solve some of these problems that we began to explore the possibilities of synthesis.

We must remember now that this situation, even with the help of synthesis, can still exist, and quite often we shall find complex subjects only some of whose ideas or aspects can be dealt with by the scheme. For example

THE TRANSPORT OF VOTERS TO THE POLLS IN BRITISH
ELECTIONS

(which has, in fact, been the subject of a government publication) presents us with just such a problem. This specific topic does not exist in DC, and the nearest general heading is 324.242 VOTING PROCE-DURE. GEOGRAPHICAL SUBDIVISION in this class, however, is given the special places 324.4-.9 because of its significance, so BRITISH ELECTIONS already has a number 324.42. These two numbers cannot be combined, and the user of the scheme must decide whether he wants his material in this field collected by the problems of SUFFRAGE AND ELECTIONS, regardless of country, or by COUNTRY, knowing that there is no way of arranging the material by PROBLEM under each country.

What we must do in such cases is to analyse the complex subject and recognise its constituent ideas and aspects. Then we must select the MOST IMPORTANT SUBDIVISIONS, as many as can be classified by the scheme, and ignore the others.

At one time DC had elaborate but ungainly arrangements to combine special subdivisions, common subdivisions and geographical subdivisions, but these have now been rejected by the editors, with a few exceptions. At this stage, authority in classifying passes out of the hands of the scheme into those of the classifier.

FROM NOW ON IT IS UP TO YOU

AN ALPHABETICAL INDEX TO THE EXAMPLES TO BE CLASSIFIED